THE ESSENTIAL GUIDE TO

Becoming a
MASTER STUDENT

5e

Based on Dave Ellis' *Becoming a Master Student*

Contributing Editor:
Doug Toft

Australia • Brazil • Mexico • Singapore • United Kingdom • United States

CENGAGE

The Essential Guide to Becoming a Master Student, **Fifth Edition**
Dave Ellis

Product Director: Lauren Murphy

Product Manager: Sarah Seymour

Sr. Content Development Manager:
Alexandria Brady

Product Assistant: Emily Wiener

Marketing Manager: Allison Moghaddasi

Senior Content Project Manager: Margaret
Park Bridges

Manufacturing Planner: Beverly Breslin

IP Analyst: Ann Hoffman

Senior IP Project Manager: Kathryn
Kucharek

Production Service: MPS Limited

Compositor: MPS Limited

Art Director: Diana Graham

Text Designer: Diana Graham

Cover Designer: Diana Graham

Cover Image: iStockPhoto.com/Rawpixel

© 2019, 2016, 2013 Cengage Learning, Inc.

Unless otherwise noted, all content is © Cengage

For product information and technology assistance, contact us at
Cengage Customer & Sales Support, 1-800-354-9706.
For permission to use material from this text or product,
submit all requests online at **www.cengage.com/permissions**.
Further permissions questions can be emailed to
permissionrequest@cengage.com.

Library of Congress Control Number: 2017938976

Student Edition:
ISBN: 978-1-337-55635-4

Loose-leaf Edition:
ISBN: 978-1-337-56371-0

Cengage
20 Channel Center Street
Boston, MA 02210
USA

Cengage is a leading provider of customized learning solutions with employees residing in nearly 40 different countries and sales in more than 125 countries around the world. Find your local representative at **www.cengage.com**.

Cengage products are represented in Canada by Nelson Education, Ltd.

To learn more about Cengage platforms and services, visit **www.cengage.com**.

Purchase any of our products at your local college store or at our preferred online store **www.cengagebrain.com**.

Printed in the United States of America
Print Number: 01   Print Year: 2017

Contents

WHAT'S NEW

GLOBAL UPDATES

- A more streamlined design allows articles to flow, and eliminates the distracting clutter in the chapter openers.
- Chapter openers now have a full table of contents for easier navigation.
- Many updates to the Why & How sections and "Do you have a minute?" in the chapter openers.

CHAPTER-BY-CHAPTER UPDATES

Introduction: Getting Involved
- "The Master Student Process" now defines Discovery/Intention/Action.
- Updated Skills Snapshot to include more on building habits.

Chapter 1: Using Your Learning Styles
- Expanded "Using your Learning Style Profile to succeed."

Chapter 2: Taking Charge of Your Time & Money
- New article "Setting and achieving goals."
- Reduced number of "Do you have a minute?" boxes in article "Time management essentials" added new one to replace three.
- Heavily revised "Put an end to money worries" to include more suggestions on earning more and spending less.

Chapter 3: Achieving Your Purpose for Reading
- Reorganization of chapter to keep the flow of the "Phase" articles.
- Heavily revised "Phase 3."
- New sidebar "The magic of metacognition."

Chapter 4: Participating in Class & Taking Notes
- Expanded "Play with note-taking formats."

Chapter 5: Maximizing Your Memory & Mastering Tests
- Updated "Be ready for your next test" to include information on digital flashcards, expanded on planning reviews.
- Replaced technique #7 in "12 memory techniques" and added an action to #8.
- Modified "Five things to do with your study group" to be more active around self-testing.
- New closing "Do you have a minute?"

Chapter 6: Developing Information Literacy
- Extensively revised to focus on information literacy, all content is mostly new or revised.

Chapter 7: Thinking Critically & Communicating Your Ideas
- New "Do you have a minute?" following "Becoming a critical thinker."
- Revised Skills Snapshot.

Chapter 8: Creating Positive Relationships in a Diverse World
- Revised "Thriving in a diverse world" to include reflection on privilege and prejudice.
- Revised "Managing conflict" article to include more about internal motivations.

Chapter 9: Choosing Greater Health
- Heavy revision of "Wake up to health."
- Updated list of recommendations from the United States Department of Agriculture (USDA) in "Choose your fuel."
- Revision to "Journal Entry: Asking for help."

Chapter 10: Choosing Your Major & Planning Your Career
- Replaced Technology skills with Information Literacy skills in "50 transferable skills."
- Revised Skills Snapshot.

In addition, the accompanying MindTap includes improved grading, additional help tools and assignments, increased flexibility for customizing your course, and more. Visit www.cengage.com for more information. ✖

DISCOVERY
& INTENTION
STATEMENT

GUIDELINES

DISCOVERY STATEMENTS

- [ ] Record the specifics about your thoughts, feelings, and behavior.

- [ ] Notice your thoughts, observe your actions, and record them accurately.

- [ ] Use discomfort as a signal.

- [ ] Feeling uncomfortable, bored, or tired might be a signal that you're about to do valuable work.

- [ ] Suspend judgment.

- [ ] When you are discovering yourself, be gentle.

- [ ] Tell the truth.

- [ ] The closer you get to the truth, the more powerful your Discovery Statements.

INTENTION STATEMENTS

- [ ] Make intentions positive.

- [ ] Focus on what you want rather than what you don't want.

- [ ] Make intentions observable.

- [ ] Be specific about your intentions.

- [ ] Make intentions small and achievable.

- [ ] Break large goals into small, specific tasks that can be accomplished quickly.

- [ ] Set timelines.

- [ ] Set a precise due date for tasks you intend to do.

- [ ] Move from intention to action.

If you want new results in your life, then take action. ✂

Getting Involved

why

You can ease your transition to higher education and set up a lifelong pattern of success by starting with some key strategies.

how

Take a few minutes to skim this chapter. Look at every page. Scan headlines. Notice pictures, forms, charts, and diagrams. Find three suggestions that look especially useful. Highlight or underline them and write a note to yourself about when and where you plan to use them.

what if...

I could use the ideas in this text to consistently get what I want in all areas of my life?

what is included ...

do you have a minute?

Take a minute to make a list of anything about your life that's nagging at you as incomplete or unresolved. Possibilities for this list include:

- Longstanding problems that are still not solved
- Projects that you'd like to finish and haven't yet started
- Tasks that you've been putting off
- Habits that you'd like to stop—or start

Save this list and refer to it as you read and do this chapter. *Everything you wrote down is a clue that something is important to you.* This chapter is filled with strategies for getting clear about what you want and taking immediate steps to get it.

Discover what you want

Imagine a man who tries to buy a plane ticket for his next vacation, with no destination in mind. He pulls out his iPad and logs in to his favorite website for trip planning. He gets a screen that prompts him for details about his destination. And he leaves all the fields blank.

"I'm not fussy," says the would-be vacationer. "I just want to get away. I'll just accept whatever the computer coughs up."

Compare this person to another traveler who books a flight to Ixtapa, Mexico, departing on Saturday, March 23, and returning Sunday, April 7—window seat, first class, and vegetarian meals.

Now, ask yourself which traveler is more likely to end up with a vacation that he'll enjoy.

The same principle applies in any area of life. Knowing where we want to go increases the probability that we will arrive at our destination. Discovering what we want makes it more likely that we'll attain it.

Okay, so the example about the traveler with no destination is far-fetched. Before you dismiss it, though, do an informal experiment: Ask three other students what they want to get out of their education. Be prepared for hemming, hawing, and vague generalities.

This is amazing, considering the stakes involved. Students routinely invest years of their lives and thousands of dollars, with only a hazy idea of their destination in life.

Now suppose that you asked someone what she wanted from her education, and you got this answer: "I plan to get a degree in journalism, with double minors in earth science and Portuguese, so I can work as a reporter covering the environment in Brazil." The details of a person's vision offer clues to his or her skills and sense of purpose.

Another clue is the presence of "stretch goals"—those that are big *and* achievable. A 40-year-old might spend years talking about his desire to be a professional athlete someday. Chances are, that's no longer achievable. However, setting a goal to lose 10 pounds by playing basketball at the gym three days a week is another matter. That's a stretch—a challenge. It's also doable.

Discovering what you want helps you succeed in higher education. Many students quit school simply because they are unsure about what they want from it. With well-defined goals in mind, you can look for connections between what you want and what you study. The more connections, the more likely you'll stay in school—and get what you want in every area of life. ▪

Making the transition to higher education:
SIX THINGS YOU CAN DO NOW

People who are new to higher education get a common piece of advice: "You'll get the hang of being in school. Just give it time." However, you can often *reduce* your transition time—and your initial discomfort—with the following strategies.

1. Plug into resources. A supercharger increases the air supply to an internal combustion engine. The resulting difference in power can be dramatic. You can make just as powerful a difference in your education if you supercharge it by using all of the resources available to students. In this case, your "air supply" includes people, campus clubs and organizations, and school and community services.

Of all resources, people are the most important. You can isolate yourself, study hard, and get a good education. However, doing this is not the most powerful use of your tuition money. When you establish relationships with teachers, staff members, fellow students, and potential employers, you can get a *great* education.

Accessing resources is especially important if you are the first person in your family to enter higher education. As a first-generation student, you are having experiences that people in your family may not understand. Talk to your relatives about your activities at school. If they ask how they can help you, give specific answers. Also ask your instructors about programs for first-generation students on your campus.

2. Meet with your academic advisor. One person in particular—your academic advisor—can help you access resources and make the transition to higher education. Meet with this person regularly. Advisors generally know about course requirements, options for declaring majors, and the resources available at your school. Peer advisors might also be available.

3. Show up for class. The amount that you pay in tuition and fees makes a powerful argument for going to classes regularly. In large part, the material that you're tested on comes from events that take place in class.

Showing up for class occurs on two levels. The most visible level is being physically present in the classroom. Even more important, though, is showing up mentally. This kind of attendance includes taking detailed notes, asking questions, and contributing to class discussions.

4. Be willing to rethink how you learn. Many students arrive in higher education with study skills that were honed for high school. They underestimate how long it takes to complete assignments and prepare for tests. These students get an unpleasant surprise when their grades take a hit.

To avoid this fate, embrace new strategies for learning. Don't prepare for tests by simply memorizing isolated facts. Instead, relate facts to the big ideas in your courses. State those ideas in your own words. Give examples based on personal experience whenever possible, and explain how you would apply the ideas. The strategies presented in this text can help you do all of these things.

5. Take the initiative in meeting new people. Realize that most of the people in this new world of higher education are waiting to be welcomed. You can help them and help yourself at the same time. Introduce yourself to classmates and instructors. Just before or after class is a good time.

6. Admit your feelings—whatever they are. School can be an intimidating experience for new students. People of diverse cultures, adult learners, commuters, and people with disabilities may feel excluded. Feelings of anxiety, isolation, and homesickness are common among students.

Those emotions are common among new students, and there's nothing wrong with them. Simply admitting the truth about how you feel—to yourself and to someone else—can help you cope. And you can almost always do something constructive in the present moment, no matter how you feel.

If your feelings about the transition to higher education make it hard for you to carry out the activities of daily life—going to class, working, studying, and relating to people—then get professional help. Start with a counselor at the student health service on your campus. The mere act of seeking help can make a difference. ✖

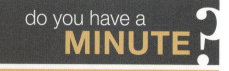
Master student
QUALITIES

This text is about something that cannot be taught. It's about becoming a master student.

Oliver Cleve/Getty Images

Mastery means attaining a level of skill that goes beyond technique. For a master, work is effortless; struggle evaporates. The master carpenter is so familiar with her tools that they are part of her. To a master chef, utensils are old friends. Because these masters don't have to think about the details of the process, they bring more of themselves to their work.

Often, the result of mastery is a sense of profound satisfaction, well-being, and timelessness. Distractions fade. Time stops. Work becomes play. After hours of patient practice, after setting clear goals and getting precise feedback, the master has learned to be fully in control.

At the same time, he lets go of control. Results happen without effort, struggle, or worry. Work seems self-propelled. The master is in control by being out of control. He lets go and allows the creative process to take over. That's why after a spectacular performance by an athlete or artist, observers often say, "He played full out—and made it look like he wasn't even trying."

Likewise, the master student is one who makes learning look easy. She works hard without seeming to make any effort. She's relaxed *and* alert, disciplined *and* spontaneous, focused *and* fun-loving.

You might say that those statements don't make sense. Actually, mastery does *not* make sense. It cannot be captured with words. It defies analysis. Mastery cannot be taught. It can only be learned and experienced.

Master students share certain qualities. Though they imply various strategies for learning, they ultimately go beyond what people *do*. Master student qualities are values. They are ways of *being* exceptional.

Following is a list of master student qualities. Remember that the list is not complete. It merely points in a direction.

As you read the following list, look to yourself. Put a check mark next to each quality that you've already demonstrated. Put another mark—say, an exclamation point—next to each quality you want to actively work on possessing. This is not a test. It is simply a chance to celebrate what you've accomplished so far—and to start thinking about what's possible for your future.

☐ **Inquisitive.** The master student is curious about everything. By posing questions, she can generate interest in the most mundane, humdrum situations.

☐ **Able to focus attention.** Watch a 2-year-old at play. Pay attention to his eyes. The wide-eyed look reveals an energy and a capacity for amazement that keep his attention absolutely focused in the here and now. The master student's focused attention has this kind of childlike quality. The world, to a master student, is always new.

☐ **Willing to change.** The unknown does not frighten the master student. In fact, she welcomes it—even the unknown in herself.

☐ **Able to organize and sort.** The master student can take a large body of information and sift through it to discover relationships.

☐ **Competent.** Mastery of skills is important to the master student. When he learns mathematical formulas, he studies them until they become second nature. He also is able to apply what he learns to new and different situations.

☐ **Joyful.** More often than not, the master student is seen with a smile on her face—sometimes a smile at nothing in particular other than amazement at the world and her experience of it.

☐ **Able to suspend judgment.** The master student has opinions, and he is able to let go of them when appropriate. He can quiet his internal dialogue and listen to opposing viewpoints.

☐ **Energetic.** Notice the student with a spring in her step, the one who is enthusiastic and involved in class. When she reads, she often sits on the very edge of her chair, and she plays with the same intensity.

☐ **Well.** The master student treats his body with respect. He tends to his health at all levels—body, mind, and spirit.

☐ **Self-aware.** The master student is willing to evaluate himself and his behavior. He regularly tells the truth about his strengths and those aspects that could be improved.

☐ **Responsible.** There is a difference between responsibility and blame, and the master student knows it well. She is willing to take responsibility for everything in her life—even for events that most people would blame on others. For example, if a master student takes a required class that most students consider boring, she chooses to take responsibility for her interest level. She looks for ways to link the class to one of her goals. She sees the class as an opportunity to experiment with new study techniques that will enhance her performance in any course. She remembers that by choosing her thoughts and behaviors, she can create interesting classes, enjoyable relationships, fulfilling work experiences, or just about anything else she wants.

☐ **Willing to take risks.** The master student often takes on projects with no guarantee of success. He participates in class dialogues at the risk of looking foolish. He tackles difficult subjects in term papers. He welcomes the risk of a challenging course.

☐ **Willing to participate.** Don't look for the master student on the sidelines. She's in the game. She is a team player who can be counted on. She is engaged at school, at work, and with friends and family. She is willing to make a commitment and to follow through on it.

☐ **A generalist.** The master student seeks out experiences that give him a broad range of knowledge. He can apply this knowledge to his special interests, creating new ideas in the process.

☐ **Courageous.** The master student admits her fear and fully experiences it. For example, she will approach a tough exam as an opportunity to explore feelings of anxiety and tension related to the pressure to perform. She does not deny fear; she embraces it.

☐ **Self-directed.** Rewards or punishments provided by others do not motivate the master student. His desire to learn comes from within, and his goals come from himself. He competes like a star athlete—not to defeat other people, but to push himself to the next level of excellence.

- [ ] **Spontaneous.** The master student is truly in the here and now. She is able to respond to the moment in fresh, surprising, and unplanned ways.

- [ ] **Relaxed about grades.** Grades make the master student neither depressed nor euphoric. He recognizes that sometimes grades are important. At the same time, he does not measure his worth as a human being by the grades he receives.

- [ ] **"Tech" savvy.** A master student defines *technology* as any tool that's used to achieve a human purpose. From this point of view, computers become tools for deeper learning, higher productivity, and greater success. She knows when to go online—and when to go offline so that she can fully engage with people face-to-face.

- [ ] **Intuitive.** The master student has an inner sense that cannot be explained by logic alone. He trusts his "gut instincts" as well as his mind.

- [ ] **Creative.** Where others see dull details and trivia, the master student sees opportunities to create. The master student is creative in every aspect of her life.

- [ ] **Willing to work.** Once inspired, the master student is willing to follow through with sweat. He knows that deep learning involves persistence and effort. When in high gear, the master student works with the intensity of a child at play.

- [ ] **Willing to be uncomfortable.** The master student does not place comfort first. When discomfort is necessary to reach a goal, he is willing to experience it. He can endure personal hardships and can look at unpleasant things with detachment.

- [ ] **Optimistic.** The master student sees setbacks as temporary and isolated, knowing that she can choose her response to any circumstance. Instead of believing that her abilities are fixed at birth, she sees herself as capable of change, growth, and mastery.

- [ ] **Willing to laugh.** The master student might laugh at any moment, and his sense of humor includes the ability to laugh at himself.

- [ ] **Hungry.** Human beings begin life with a natural appetite for knowledge. The master student taps that hunger, and it gives her a desire to learn for the sake of learning.

- [ ] **Caring.** A master student cares about knowledge and has a passion for ideas. She also cares about people and appreciates learning from others. She collaborates on projects and thrives on teams. She flourishes in a community that values win–win outcomes, cooperation, and love. ✴

Get the most out of the
ESSENTIAL GUIDE PROGRAM

The purpose of this text is to help you make a successful transition to higher education by setting up a path to mastery that will last the rest of your life. And this text is worthless—*if reading it is all you do*. You'll get your money's worth only if you actively use the ideas that are presented in these pages.

The author of *Becoming a Master Student* didn't like traditional textbooks. They put him to sleep. So he chose to create a different kind of book. You're holding the result in your hands.

Nothing in this text appears by accident. Every element on every page serves as a prompt to take ideas and put them into action.

Articles are the backbone of this text. You're reading one right now. Articles are important because *The*

Essential Guide to Becoming a Master Student is designed to look like a magazine rather than a textbook.

Most magazines are filled with advertisements. So is this text. The difference is that you won't find any glossy photos of celebrities or consumer products. Instead, the articles are self-contained "advertisements" for tips, tools, strategies, and techniques that you can use immediately. You can read any article from any chapter in any order at any time. If you read each chapter from start to finish, you'll gain the advantage of seeing how the key concepts fit together.

A **Master Student Map** begins each chapter. Think of it as a GPS device for ideas. Each chapter takes you on a journey, and the Master Student Map is your guide. You can orient yourself for maximum learning every time you open this text by asking the four questions listed in the Map: *Why? What? How?* and *What if?* Those four questions are keys to learning anything.

There's a **Power Process** in each chapter. These are suggestions to play with your perspective on the world so that it becomes easier to use the ideas suggested in articles. Students often refer to the Power Processes as their favorite part of the text. Approach them with a sense of possibility.

Journal Entries are just as essential. These are invitations for you to discover what you want in life and how you intend to get it.

A **Skills Snapshot** ends each chapter. These connect with the **Discovery** Wheel included later in this chapter. Like the Discovery Wheel, the Skills Snapshots invite you to tell the truth in a nonjudgmental way about where you stand today in your path to becoming a Master Student.

One major theme of this book is time management—a challenge for most students who are new to higher education. Fortunately, time management does not have to take much time. Look for **Do you have a minute?** boxes in every chapter for suggestions that take only about 60 seconds to do. ✂

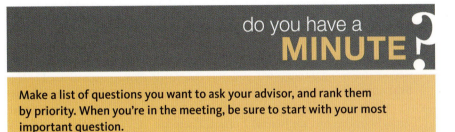

do you have a MINUTE?

Make a list of questions you want to ask your advisor, and rank them by priority. When you're in the meeting, be sure to start with your most important question.

DISCOVERY STATEMENT   journal entry **1**

Declare what you want

Review the articles you have read so far in this chapter. Then use this Journal Entry to start experiencing the master student process—the ongoing cycle of discovery, intention, and action.

Brainstorm many possible ways to complete this sentence: *I discovered that what I want most from my education is . . .* When you're done, choose the ending that feels best to you and write it down.

I discovered that what I want most from my education is . . .

The Master Student
PROCESS

Success is no mystery. Successful people have left clues—*many* clues, in fact. There are thousands of articles and books that give tools, tips, techniques, and strategies for success. Do an Internet search on *success* and you'll get over 300 million results.

If that sounds overwhelming, don't worry. Success is simply the process of setting and achieving goals. And the essentials of that process can be described in three words: *Discovery. Intention. Action.* They work together in phases:

- Discovery—observing your thoughts, feelings, behaviors, and current circumstances
- Intention—choosing new outcomes that you'd like to create
- Action—following through with your intentions with new behaviors

Throughout this text are Journal Entries. These are invitations to reflect and write. They are also your chance to personally experience success through the cycle of discovery, intention, and action.

WRITE DISCOVERY STATEMENTS

The first stage is a Discovery Statement. These often begin with a prompt, such as "I discovered that . . ." Here is an opportunity to reflect on "where you are." Discovery Statements describe your current strengths and areas for improvement. Discovery Statements can also be descriptions of your feelings, thoughts, and behavior. Whenever you get an "aha!" moment—a flash of insight or a sudden solution to a problem—put it in a Discovery Statement. To write effective Discovery Statements, remember the following.

Record the specifics about your thoughts, feelings, and behavior. Thoughts include inner voices. We talk to ourselves constantly in our head. When internal chatter gets in the way, write down what you tell yourself. If this seems difficult at first, just start writing. The act of writing can trigger a flood of thoughts.

Thoughts also include mental pictures. These are especially powerful. Picturing yourself flunking a test is like a rehearsal to do just that. One way to take away the power of negative images is to describe them in detail.

Also notice how you feel when you function well. Use Discovery Statements to pinpoint exactly where and when you learn most effectively.

In addition, observe your emotions and actions, and record the facts. If you spent 90 minutes chatting online with a favorite cousin instead of reading your anatomy text,
write about it. Include the details—when you did it, where you did it, and how it felt.

Use discomfort as a signal. When you approach a hard task, such as a difficult math problem, notice your physical sensations. These might include a churning stomach, shallow breathing, and yawning. Feeling uncomfortable, bored, or tired can be a signal that you're about to do valuable work. Stick with it. Write about it. Tell yourself you can handle the discomfort just a little bit longer. You will be rewarded with a new insight.

Suspend judgment. As you learn about yourself, be gentle. Suspend self-judgment. If you continually judge your behaviors as "bad" or "stupid," your mind will quit making discoveries rather than put up with abuse. For your own benefit, be kind to yourself.

Tell the truth. Suspending judgment helps you tell the truth about yourself. "The truth will set you free" is a saying that endures for a reason. The closer you get to the truth, the more powerful your Discovery Statements. And if you notice that you are avoiding the truth, don't blame yourself. Just tell the truth about it.

WRITE INTENTION STATEMENTS

Intention Statements can be used to alter your course. They are statements of your commitment to do a specific task or achieve a goal. Discovery Statements promote awareness, whereas Intention Statements are blueprints for action. The two processes reinforce each other.

Make intentions positive. The purpose of writing Intention Statements is to focus on what you *do* want rather than what you *don't* want. Instead of writing "I will not fall asleep while studying chemistry," write, "I intend to stay awake when studying chemistry." Also avoid the word *try*. Trying is not doing. When we hedge our bets with *try*, we can always tell ourselves, "Well, I *tried* to stay awake."

Make intentions observable. Rather than writing "I intend to work harder on my history assignments," write, "I intend to review my class notes daily and make summary sheets of my reading."

Integrity . . . making time for what matters most

Living with integrity is a challenge. For example, people might tell you that they're open-minded—and then get angry when you disagree with them. Students might say that they value education—and then skip classes to party. When our words and actions get out of alignment, then we stop getting the results that we want.

One solution is to define your values as high-priority activities. In your journal, brainstorm ways to complete this sentence: *It's extremely important that I make time for . . .* Then use your answers to set goals, schedule events, and write daily to-do lists. This strategy translates your values into plans that directly affect the way you manage time.

For example, perhaps it's important for you to stay healthy. Then you can set goals to exercise regularly and manage your weight. In turn, those goals can show up as items on your to-do list and calendar—commitments to go to the gym, take an aerobics class, and include low-fat foods on your grocery list.

The ultimate time management skill is to define your values and align your actions.

Make intentions small and achievable. Break large goals into small, specific tasks that can be accomplished quickly. Small and simple changes in behavior—when practiced consistently over time—can have large and lasting effects.

When setting your goals, anticipate self-sabotage. Be aware of what you might do, consciously or unconsciously, to undermine your best intentions. Also be careful about intentions that depend on other people. If you intend for your study group to complete an assignment by Monday, then your success depends on the students in the group. Likewise, you can support your group's success by following through on your own stated intentions.

Set time lines. For example, if you are assigned a paper to write, break the assignment into small tasks and set a precise due date for each one: "I intend to select a topic for my paper by 9 a.m. Wednesday."

ACT NOW!

Carefully crafted Discovery Statements are a beauty to behold. Precise Intention Statements can inspire awe. But neither will be of much use until you put them into action. This is where the magic happens.

Life responds to what you *do*. Successful people are those who consistently produce the results that they want. And results follow from specific, consistent behaviors. If you want new results in your life, then take new actions.

Get physical. This phase of the process is about moving from thinking to doing. Translate goals into physical actions that would show up on a video recording. Get your legs, arms, and mouth moving.

Welcome discomfort. Changing your behavior might lead to feelings of discomfort. Instead of going back to your old behaviors, befriend the yucky feelings. Taking action has a way of dissolving discomfort.

When you get stuck, tell the truth about it. As you become a student of human behavior, you'll see people expecting new results from old behaviors—and then wondering why they feel stuck. Don't be surprised if you discover this tendency in yourself. Just tell the truth about it, review your intentions, and take your next action.

REPEAT THE CYCLE

The process of discovery, intention, and action is a continuous cycle. First, you write Discovery Statements about where you are now. Next, you write Intention Statements about where you want to be and the specific steps you will take to get there. Follow up with action—the sooner, the better.

Then start the cycle again. Write Discovery Statements about whether you act on your Intention Statements—and what you learn in the process. Follow up with more Intention Statements about what you will do differently in the future. Then move into action and describe what happens next.

This process never ends. Each time you repeat the cycle, you get new results. Your actions become a little more aligned with your intentions, and your intentions more accurately reflect your discoveries. Over time, these small corrections add up. Your life shifts in significant ways as you move in the direction of your dreams. ✶

do you have a MINUTE?

Write an Intention Statement to create a new habit. Make it small—a 60-second task such as flossing one tooth after you brush your teeth or doing one yoga stretch after you get out of bed in the morning. You'll find that such behaviors tend to expand naturally once you turn them into habits.

The Discovery Wheel

The Discovery Wheel is an opportunity to tell the truth about the kind of person you are—and the kind of person you want to become.

This tool is based on a fundamental idea: Success in any area of life starts with telling the truth about what is working—and what isn't—in our lives right now. When we acknowledge our strengths, we gain an accurate picture of what we can accomplish. When we admit that we have a problem, we free up energy to find a solution. It's that simple.

The Discovery Wheel gives you an opportunity to sit back for a few minutes and think about yourself. This is not a test. There are no trick questions. There are no grades. The answers you provide will have meaning only for you.

HOW THE DISCOVERY WHEEL WORKS

By doing the Discovery Wheel, you can gain awareness of your current behaviors—especially the kinds of behaviors that affect your success in school. With this knowledge, you can choose new behaviors and start to enjoy new results in your life.

During this exercise, you fill in a circle similar to the one shown in Figure I.1. The closer the shading comes to the outer edge of the circle, the higher your evaluation of a

5 points	This statement is always or almost always true of me.
4 points	This statement is often true of me.
3 points	This statement is true of me about half the time.
2 points	This statement is seldom true of me.
1 point	This statement is never or almost never true of me.

specific skill. In the example below, the student has rated her reading skills low and her note-taking skills high.

The terms *high* and *low* are not positive or negative judgments. When doing the Discovery Wheel, you are just making observations about yourself. You're like a scientist running an experiment. You are just collecting data and

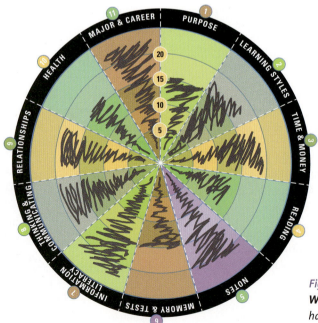

Figure I.1 Sample Discovery Wheel. *Notice how this student has rated her reading skills low and her note-taking skills high.*

recording the facts. You're not evaluating yourself as good or bad.

Remember that the Discovery Wheel is not a permanent picture of who you are. It is a picture of what you're doing right now. You'll do this exercise again, near the end. Also, the Skills Snapshot at the end of each chapter is like a mini-Discovery Wheel that allows you to update your self-evaluations.

In short, you will have many chances to measure your progress. So be honest about where you are right now.

To succeed at this exercise, tell the truth about your strengths. This is no time for modesty! Also, lighten up and be willing to laugh at yourself. A little humor can make it easier to tell the truth about your areas for improvement.

To begin this exercise, read the following statements and give yourself points for each one, based on the point system described. Then add up your point total for each category and shade the Discovery Wheel to the appropriate level.

1 Purpose

_____ I can clearly state my overall purpose in life.
_____ I can explain how school relates to what I plan to do after I graduate.
_____ I capture key insights in writing and clarify exactly how I intend to act on them.
_____ I am skilled at making transitions.
_____ I seek out and use resources to support my success.
_____ **Total Score: Purpose**

2 Learning Styles

_____ I enjoy learning.
_____ I make a habit of assessing my personal strengths and areas for improvement.
_____ I monitor my understanding of a topic and change learning strategies if I get confused.
_____ I use my knowledge of various learning styles to support my success in school.
_____ I am open to different points of view on almost any topic.
_____ **Total Score: Learning Styles**

3 Time & Money

_____ I can clearly describe what I want to experience in major areas of my life, including career, relationships, financial well-being, and health.
_____ I set goals and periodically review them.
_____ I plan each day and often accomplish what I plan.
_____ I will have enough money to complete my education.
_____ I monitor my income, keep track of my expenses, and live within my means.
_____ **Total Score: Time & Money**

4 Reading

_____ I ask myself questions about what I'm reading.
_____ I preview and review reading assignments.
_____ I relate what I read to my life.
_____ I select strategies to fit the type of material I'm reading.
_____ When I don't understand what I'm reading, I note my questions and find answers.
_____ **Total Score: Reading**

5 Notes

_____ When I am in class, I focus my attention.
_____ I take notes in class.
_____ I can explain various methods for taking notes, and I choose those that work best for me.
_____ I distinguish key points from supporting examples.
_____ I put important concepts into my own words.
_____ **Total Score: Notes**

6 Memory & Tests

_____ The way that I talk about my value as a person is independent of my grades.
_____ I often succeed at predicting test questions.
_____ I review for tests throughout the term.
_____ I manage my time during tests.
_____ I use techniques to remember key facts and ideas.
_____ **Total Score: Memory & Tests**

7 Information Literacy

_____ I choose appropriate topics for research projects.

_____ I translate topics into questions that effectively guide my research.

_____ I find credible sources of information to answer my questions.

_____ I think critically about information that I find.

_____ I translate the results of my research into effective speaking and writing.

_____ **Total Score: Information Literacy**

8 Thinking & Communicating

_____ I use brainstorming to generate solutions to problems.

_____ I can detect common errors in logic and gaps in evidence.

_____ When researching, I find relevant facts and properly credit their sources.

_____ I edit my writing for clarity, accuracy, and coherence.

_____ I prepare and deliver effective presentations.

_____ **Total Score: Thinking & Communicating**

9 Relationships

_____ Other people tell me that I am a good listener.

_____ I communicate my upsets without blaming others.

_____ I build rewarding relationships with people from other backgrounds.

_____ I effectively resolve conflict.

_____ I participate effectively in teams and take on leadership roles.

_____ **Total Score: Relationships**

10 Health

_____ I have enough energy to study, attend classes, and enjoy other areas of my life.

_____ The way I eat supports my long-term health.

_____ I exercise regularly.

_____ I can cope effectively with stress.

_____ I'm in control of alcohol or other drugs I put in my body.

_____ **Total Score: Health**

11 Major & Career

_____ I have a detailed list of my skills.

_____ I have a written career plan and update it regularly.

_____ I use the career-planning services at my school.

_____ I participate in internships, extracurricular activities, information interviews, and on-the-job experiences to test and refine my career plan.

_____ I have declared a major related to my interests, skills, and core values.

_____ **Total Score: Major & Career**

Using the total score from each category, shade in each section of the blank Discovery Wheel in Figure I.2. If you want, use different colors. For example, you could use green for areas you want to work on.

REFLECT ON YOUR DISCOVERY WHEEL
Now that you have completed your Discovery Wheel, spend a few minutes with it. Get a sense of its weight, shape, and balance. How would it sound if it rolled down a hill?

Next, complete the following sentences. Just write down whatever comes to mind. Remember, this is not a test.

The two areas in which I am strongest are . . .

The two areas in which I most want to improve are . . .

Finally, take about 15 minutes to do a "textbook reconnaissance" much like the preview you did for this chapter. First,

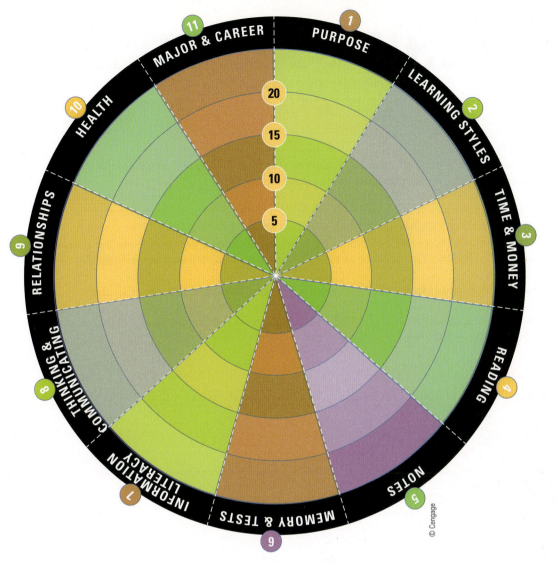

Figure I.2 **Your Discovery Wheel.**

scan the Table of Contents. Next, look at every page. Move quickly. Skim the words in bold print. Glance at pictures. Look for suggestions that can help with behaviors you want to change. Find five such suggestions that look especially interesting to you. Then write a short description of each idea and a page number or location in the text where you can find out more.

SKILLS *snapshot*

Introduction

To get the most value from this text, take the suggestions that work for you and turn them into habits. In his book *The Power of Habit*, Charles Duhigg explains that any habit has three elements:[1]

- **Routine.** This is a behavior that we repeat, usually without thinking. Examples are taking a second helping at dinner, biting fingernails, or automatically hitting the "snooze" button when the alarm goes off in the morning.
- **Cue.** Also known as a *trigger*, this is an event that occurs right before we perform the routine. It might be an internal event, such as a change in mood. Or it could be an external event, such as seeing an advertisement that triggers cravings for a chocolate chip cookie.
- **Reward.** This is the payoff for the routine—usually a feeling of pleasure or a reduction in stress.

Taken together, these elements form a habit loop: You perceive a *cue* and then perform a *routine* in order to get a *reward*. Use this Skills Snapshot to test Duhigg's ideas for yourself.

Step 1: Identify a routine.
Begin by describing one of your current routines. Describe one specific behavior that you'd like to change.

Step 2: Identify the cue.
Describe the cue for the behavior you listed in Step 1.

Step 3: Identify the reward.
Describe the reward that you get from the behavior listed in Step 1.

Step 4: Choose a new routine.
Now choose a *new* routine that you can perform in response to the cue. The challenge is to choose a behavior that offers a reward with as few disadvantages as possible. Instead of eating a chocolate chip cookie, for example, you could eat a small dish of unsweetened applesauce. This snack is naturally sweet with no added sugar. You experience a familiar pleasure with a fraction of the calories.

Describe your new routine here:

After taking action on your intention for at least one week, describe your success in doing the new routine. Also, include any ideas for your next experiment in habit change.

do you have a **MINUTE**?

Review the new routine that you just wrote. Is it something that you can do in 60 seconds or less? If not, then rethink it. List your revised routine here.

ESB Basic/Shutterstock.com

Using Your Learning Styles

why

Success starts with telling the truth about what *is* working—and what *isn't*—in your life right now.

how

Skim this chapter for three techniques that you'd like to apply in school or in your personal life during the upcoming week. Highlight those techniques and then write Intention Statements about how and when you will use those techniques.

what if...

I could start to create new outcomes in my life by accepting the way I am right now?

what is included...

do you have a minute?

Take a minute to write down a "baby step"—a task that takes 60 seconds or less—that can help you move toward completing a current project or assignment. For example, brainstorm a list of topics for a paper that you plan to write. If you can spare another minute, then do that task immediately.

Ideas are tools

There are many ideas in this text. When you first encounter them, don't believe any of them. Instead, think of the ideas as tools.

For example, you use a hammer for a purpose—to drive a nail. You don't try to figure out whether the hammer is "right." You just use it. If it works, you use it again. If it doesn't work, you get a different hammer.

People have plenty of room in their lives for different kinds of hammers, but they tend to limit their openness to different kinds of ideas. A new idea, at some level, is a threat to their very being—unlike a new hammer, which is simply a new hammer.

Most of us have a built-in desire to be right. Our ideas, we often think, represent ourselves.

Some ideas are worth dying for. But please note: This text does not contain any of those ideas. The ideas on these pages are strictly "hammers."

Imagine someone defending a hammer. Picture this person holding up a hammer and declaring, "I hold this hammer to be self-evident. Give me this hammer or give me death. Those other hammers are flawed. There are only two kinds of people in this world:

people who believe in this hammer and people who don't."

That ridiculous picture makes a point. This text is not a manifesto. It's a toolbox, and tools are meant to be used.

If you read about a tool in this text that doesn't sound "right" or one that sounds a little goofy, remember that the ideas here are for using, not necessarily for believing. Suspend your judgment. Test the idea for yourself. If it works, use it. If it doesn't, don't use it.

Any tool—a hammer, a computer program, a study technique—is designed to do a specific job. A master mechanic carries a variety of tools because no single tool works for all jobs. If you throw a tool away because it doesn't work in one situation, you won't be able to pull it out later when it's just what you need. So if an idea doesn't work for you and you are satisfied that you gave it a fair chance, don't throw it away. File it away instead. The idea might come in handy soon.

And remember, this text is not about figuring out the "right" way. Even the "ideas are tools" approach is not "right."

It's just a tool.

Anteromite/Shutterstock.com

LEARNING STYLES:

Discovering how you learn

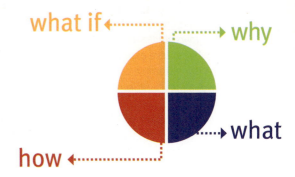

Right now, you are investing substantial amounts of time, money, and energy in your education. What you get in return for this investment depends on how well you understand the process of learning and use it to your advantage.

If you don't understand learning, you might feel bored or confused in class. After getting a low grade, you might have no idea how to respond. Over time, frustration can mount to the point where you question the value of being in school.

Some students answer that question by dropping out of school. These students lose a chance to create the life they want, and society loses the contributions of educated workers.

You can prevent that outcome. Gain strategies for going beyond boredom and confusion. Discover new options for achieving goals, solving problems, listening more fully, speaking more persuasively, and resolving conflicts between people. Start by understanding the different ways that people create meaning from their experience and change their behavior. In other words, learn about *how* you learn.

WE LEARN BY PERCEIVING AND PROCESSING

When we learn well, says psychologist David Kolb, two things happen.[1] First, we *perceive*. That is, we notice events and "take in" new experiences.

Second, we *process*. We respond to experiences in ways that help us make sense of them.

Some people especially prefer to perceive through *feeling* (also called *concrete experience*). They like to absorb information through their five senses. They learn by getting directly involved in new experiences. When solving problems, they rely on intuition as much as intellect.

Other people like to perceive by *thinking* (also called *abstract conceptualization*). They analyze, intellectualize, and create theories. Often these people take a scientific approach to problem solving and excel in traditional classrooms.

Some people prefer to process by *watching* (also called *reflective observation*). They prefer to stand back, watch what is going on, and reflect on it. They consider several points of view as they attempt to make sense of things and generate many ideas about how something happens.

Other people like to process by *doing* (also called *active experimentation*). They prefer to jump in and start doing things immediately. These people are willing to take risks as they attempt to make sense of things. They are results oriented and look for practical ways to apply what they learn.

PERCEIVING AND PROCESSING—AN EXAMPLE

Suppose that you get a new cell phone. It has more features than any phone you've used before. You have many options for learning how to use it. For example:

- Just get your hands on the phone right away, press some buttons, and see whether you can dial a number or send a text message.
- Read the instruction manual and view help screens on the phone before you try to make a call.
- Recall experiences you've had with phones in the past and what you've learned by watching other people use their cell phones.
- Ask a friend who owns the same type of phone to coach you as you experiment with making calls and sending messages.

These actions illustrate the different approaches to learning:

- Getting your hands on the phone right away and seeing whether you can make it work is an example of learning through *feeling* (or *concrete experience*).
- Reading the manual and help screens before you use the phone is an

example of learning through *thinking* (or *abstract conceptualization*).

- Recalling what you've experienced in the past is an example of learning through *watching* (or *reflective observation*).
- Asking a friend to coach you through a hands-on activity with the phone is an example of learning through *doing* (or *active experimentation*).

In summary, your learning style is the unique way that you blend thinking, feeling, watching, and doing. You tend to use this approach in learning anything—from cell phones to English composition to sky diving. Doing the recommended activities in this chapter will help you explore your learning style in more detail. ✄

Recall the last time you learned to use a new device such as a smartphone or appliance. Did you rely primarily on thinking, feeling, doing, or watching? Take a minute now to write down what you noticed about your learning style in a Discovery Statement.

Directions for Completing the Learning Style Inventory

To help you become more aware of learning styles, a psychologist named David Kolb developed the Learning Style Inventory (LSI). Responding to the items in the LSI can help you discover a lot about ways you learn. Following the LSI are suggestions for using the LSI results to promote your success.

The LSI is not a test. There are no right or wrong answers. Your goal is simply to develop a profile of your current learning style. So, take the LSI quickly. You might find it useful to recall a recent time when you learned something new at school, home, or work. However, do not agonize over your responses.

Note that the LSI consists of 12 sentences, each with four different endings. Read each sentence, and then rank each ending using the following scale:

4 = Most like you
3 = Second most like you
2 = Third most like you
1 = Least like you

Only use each number one time per sentence. This is a forced-choice inventory, so you must rank each ending. *Do not leave any endings blank.* Use each number only once for each question.

Read the instructions at the top of the LSI. When you understand example A, you are ready to begin.

Learning Style Inventory

Read the first sentence and its four possible endings. Put a 4 next to the ending that best describes the way you currently learn. Then continue ranking the other endings with a 3, 2, and 1, which represents the ending that is least like you. Do this for each sentence. Use the following example as a guide:

A. When I learn: **2** I am happy.   **3** I am fast.   **4** I am logical.   **1** I am careful.

Remember: **4 = Most like you**   **3 = Second most like you**   **2 = Third most like you**   **1 = Least like you**

Do not leave any endings blank. Use each number only once for each question.

1. When I learn:	_____ I like to deal with my feelings.	_____ I like to think about ideas.	_____ I like to be doing things.	_____ I like to watch and listen.
2. I learn best when:	_____ I listen and watch carefully.	_____ I rely on logical thinking.	_____ I trust my hunches and feelings.	_____ I work hard to get things done.
3. When I am learning:	_____ I tend to reason things out.	_____ I am responsible about things.	_____ I am quiet and reserved.	_____ I have strong feelings and reactions.
4. I learn by:	_____ feeling.	_____ doing.	_____ watching.	_____ thinking.
5. When I learn:	_____ I am open to new experiences.	_____ I look at all sides of issues.	_____ I like to analyze things, break them down into their parts.	_____ I like to try things out.
6. When I am learning:	_____ I am an observing person.	_____ I am an active person.	_____ I am an intuitive person.	_____ I am a logical person.
7. I learn best from:	_____ observation.	_____ personal relationships.	_____ rational theories.	_____ a chance to try out and practice.
8. When I learn:	_____ I like to see results from my work.	_____ I like ideas and theories.	_____ I take my time before acting.	_____ I feel personally involved in things.
9. I learn best when:	_____ I rely on my observations.	_____ I rely on my feelings.	_____ I can try things out for myself.	_____ I rely on my ideas.
10. When I am learning:	_____ I am a reserved person.	_____ I am an accepting person.	_____ I am a responsible person.	_____ I am a rational person.
11. When I learn:	_____ I get involved.	_____ I like to observe.	_____ I evaluate things.	_____ I like to be active
12. I learn best when:	_____ I analyze ideas.	_____ I am receptive and open-minded.	_____ I am careful.	_____ I am practical.

Scorecard

Brown F   Total _____

Teal W   Total _____

Purple T   Total _____

Orange D   Total _____

....

Grand Total _____

Scoring Your Inventory

Now that you've finished taking the LSI, you probably have some questions about what it means. You're about to discover some answers!

STEP 1 First, copy your numbers from the Learning Style Inventory to the corresponding lines on this page. When you've finished, add up all of the numbers you gave to the items marked with brown F letters. Then write down that total on your Scorecard next to "**Brown F**." Next, add up all of the numbers for "**Teal W**," "**Purple T**," and "**Orange D**." Write down those totals in the Scorecard box as well.

STEP 2 Add the four totals to arrive at a **Grand Total** and write down that figure in the Scorecard box. (*Note:* The grand total should equal 120. If you have a different amount, go back and re-add the colored letters. It was probably just an addition error.)

	First Column Ranking	Second Column Ranking	Third Column Ranking	Fourth Column Ranking
1. When I learn:	___ **F**	___ **T**	___ **D**	___ **W**
2. I learn best when:	___ **W**	___ **T**	___ **F**	___ **D**
3. When I am learning:	___ **T**	___ **D**	___ **W**	___ **F**
4. I learn by:	___ **F**	___ **D**	___ **W**	___ **T**
5. When I learn:	___ **F**	___ **W**	___ **T**	___ **D**
6. When I am learning:	___ **W**	___ **D**	___ **F**	___ **T**
7. I learn best from:	___ **W**	___ **F**	___ **T**	___ **D**
8. When I learn:	___ **D**	___ **T**	___ **W**	___ **F**
9. I learn best when:	___ **W**	___ **F**	___ **D**	___ **T**
10. When I am learning:	___ **W**	___ **F**	___ **D**	___ **T**
11. When I learn:	___ **F**	___ **W**	___ **T**	___ **D**
12. I learn best when:	___ **T**	___ **F**	___ **W**	___ **D**

Learning Style Graph

STEP 3 Transfer your totals from Step 2 to the lines on the Learning Style Graph below. On the brown (F) line, find the number that corresponds to your "**Brown F**" total from your Scorecard. Then write an X on this number. Do the same for your "**Teal W**," "**Purple T**," and "**Orange D**" totals. The graph on this page is for you to keep. The graph on the page about "*Developing all four modes of learning*" is for you to turn in to your instructor if required to do so.

STEP 4 Now draw four straight lines to connect the four X's. Then shade in the area to form a "kite." *This is your learning style profile.* (For an example, see the illustration below.) Each X that you placed on these lines indicates your preference for a different aspect of learning as described here.

F: Feeling
Concrete Experience

The number where you put your X on this line indicates your preference for learning things that have personal meaning. The higher your score on this line, the more you like to learn things that you feel are important and relevant to yourself.

W: Watching
Reflective Observation

Your number on this line indicates how important it is for you to reflect on the things you are learning. If your score is high on this line, you probably find it important to watch others as they learn about an assignment and then report on it to the class. You probably like to plan things out and take the time to make sure that you fully understand a topic.

T: Thinking
Abstract Conceptualization

Your number on this line indicates your preference for learning ideas, facts, and figures. If your score is high on this line, you probably like to absorb many concepts and gather lots of information on a new topic.

D: Doing
Active Experimentation

Your number on this line indicates your preference for applying ideas, using trial and error, and practicing what you learn. If your score is high on this line, you probably enjoy hands-on activities that allow you to test out ideas to see what works.

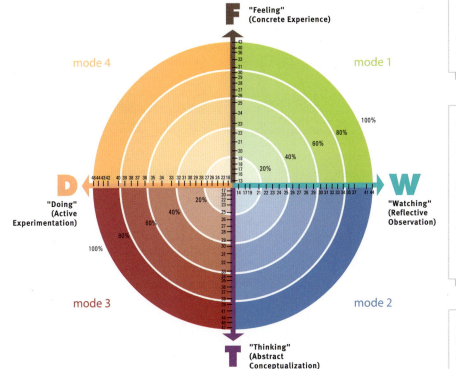

Interpreting Your Learning Style Graph

When you examine your completed Learning Style Graph, you will notice that your learning style profile (the "kite" that you drew) might be located primarily in one part of the graph. This will give you an idea of your preferred mode of learning—the kind of behaviors that feel most comfortable and familiar to you when you are learning something.

Using the descriptions below and the sample graphs, identify your preferred learning mode.

Mode 1 blends feeling and watching.
If the majority of your learning style profile is in the upper right-hand corner of the Learning Style Graph, you probably prefer Mode 1 learning. You seek a purpose for new information and a personal connection with the content. You want to know why a course matters and how it challenges or fits in with what you already know. You embrace new ideas that relate directly to your current interests and goals.

Mode 2 blends watching and thinking.
If your learning style profile is mostly in the lower right-hand corner of the Learning Style Graph, you probably prefer Mode 2 learning. You are interested in knowing what ideas or techniques are important. You seek a theory to explain events and are interested in what experts have to say. You enjoy learning lots of facts and then arranging these facts in a logical and concise manner. You break a subject down into its key elements or steps and master each one in a systematic way.

Mode 3 blends thinking and doing. If most of your learning style profile is in the lower left-hand corner of the Learning Style Graph, you probably prefer Mode 3 learning. You hunger for an opportunity to try out what you're studying. You get involved with new knowledge by testing it out. You investigate how ideas and techniques work, and you put into practice what you learn. You thrive when you have well-defined tasks, guided practice, and frequent feedback.

Mode 4 blends doing and feeling. If most of your learning style profile is in the upper left-hand corner of the Learning Style Graph, you probably prefer Mode 4 learning. You get excited about going beyond classroom assignments. You like to take what you have practiced and find other uses for it. You seek ways to apply this newly gained skill or information at your workplace or in your personal relationships.

> **It might be easier for you to remember the modes if you summarize each one as a single question:**
>
> › **Mode 1** means asking, *Why* learn this?
>
> › **Mode 2** means asking, *What* is this about?
>
> › **Mode 3** means asking, *How* does this work?
>
> › **Mode 4** means asking, *What if* I tried this in a different setting?

Combinations
Some learning style profiles combine all four modes. The profile to the left reflects a learner who is focused primarily on gathering information—*lots* of information! People with this profile tend to ask for additional facts from an instructor, or they want to know where they can go to discover more about a subject.

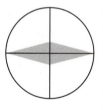

The profile to the left applies to learners who focus more on understanding what they learn and less on gathering lots of information. People with this profile prefer smaller chunks of data with plenty of time to process it. Long lectures can be difficult for these learners.

The profile to the left indicates a learner whose preferences are fairly well balanced. People with this profile can be highly adaptable and tend to excel no matter what the instructor does in the classroom.

Developing All Four Modes of Learning

Each mode of learning represents a unique blend of feeling, watching, thinking, and doing. No matter which of these you've tended to prefer, you can develop the ability to use all four modes:

- **To develop Mode 1,** ask questions that help you understand *why* it is important for you to learn about a specific topic. You might also want to form a study group.

- **To develop Mode 2,** ask questions that help you understand *what* the main points and key facts are. Also, learn a new subject in stages. For example, divide a large reading assignment into sections and then read each section carefully before moving on to the next one.

- **To develop Mode 3,** ask questions about *how* a theory relates to daily life. Also allow time to practice what you learn. You can do experiments, conduct interviews, create presentations, find a relevant work or internship experience, or even write a song that summarizes key concepts. Learn through hands-on practice.

- **To develop Mode 4,** ask *what-if* questions about ways to use what you have just learned in several different situations. Also, seek opportunities to demonstrate your understanding. You could coach a classmate about what you have learned, present findings from your research, explain how your project works, or perform your song.

Developing all four modes offers many potential benefits. For example, you can excel in many types of courses and find more opportunities to learn outside the classroom. You can expand your options for declaring a major and choosing a career. You can also work more effectively with people who learn differently from you.

In addition, you'll be able to learn from instructors no matter how they teach. Let go of statements such as "My teachers don't get me" and "The instructor doesn't teach to my learning style." Replace those excuses with attitudes such as "I am responsible for what I learn" and "I will master this subject by using several modes of learning."

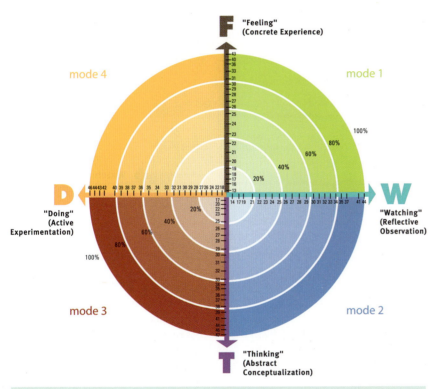

The graph on this page is here for you to turn in to your instructor if required to do so.

Balancing Your Preferences

The chart below identifies some of the natural talents people have, as well as challenges for people who have a strong preference for any one mode of learning. For example, if most of your "kite" is in Mode 2 of the Learning Style Graph, then look at the lower right-hand corner of the following chart to see whether it gives an accurate description of you.

After reviewing the description of your preferred learning mode, read all of the sections that start with the words "People with other preferred modes." These sections explain what actions you can take to become a more balanced learner.

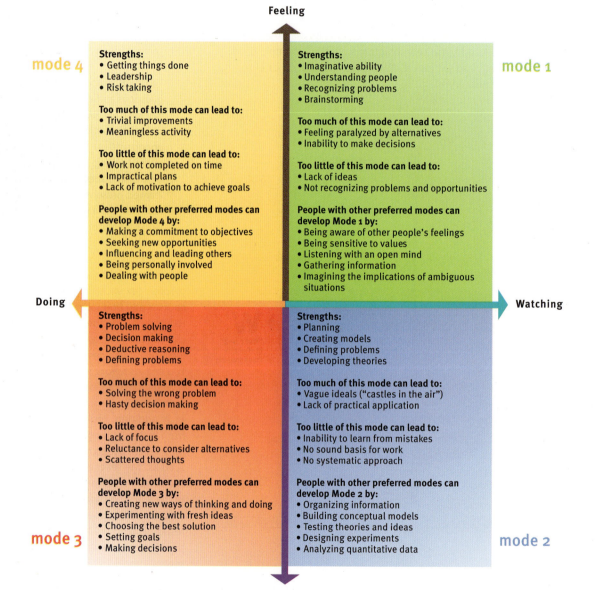

Feeling

mode 4

Strengths:
• Getting things done
• Leadership
• Risk taking

Too much of this mode can lead to:
• Trivial improvements
• Meaningless activity

Too little of this mode can lead to:
• Work not completed on time
• Impractical plans
• Lack of motivation to achieve goals

People with other preferred modes can develop Mode 4 by:
• Making a commitment to objectives
• Seeking new opportunities
• Influencing and leading others
• Being personally involved
• Dealing with people

mode 1

Strengths:
• Imaginative ability
• Understanding people
• Recognizing problems
• Brainstorming

Too much of this mode can lead to:
• Feeling paralyzed by alternatives
• Inability to make decisions

Too little of this mode can lead to:
• Lack of ideas
• Not recognizing problems and opportunities

People with other preferred modes can develop Mode 1 by:
• Being aware of other people's feelings
• Being sensitive to values
• Listening with an open mind
• Gathering information
• Imagining the implications of ambiguous situations

Doing ← → **Watching**

mode 3

Strengths:
• Problem solving
• Decision making
• Deductive reasoning
• Defining problems

Too much of this mode can lead to:
• Solving the wrong problem
• Hasty decision making

Too little of this mode can lead to:
• Lack of focus
• Reluctance to consider alternatives
• Scattered thoughts

People with other preferred modes can develop Mode 3 by:
• Creating new ways of thinking and doing
• Experimenting with fresh ideas
• Choosing the best solution
• Setting goals
• Making decisions

mode 2

Strengths:
• Planning
• Creating models
• Defining problems
• Developing theories

Too much of this mode can lead to:
• Vague ideals ("castles in the air")
• Lack of practical application

Too little of this mode can lead to:
• Inability to learn from mistakes
• No sound basis for work
• No systematic approach

People with other preferred modes can develop Mode 2 by:
• Organizing information
• Building conceptual models
• Testing theories and ideas
• Designing experiments
• Analyzing quantitative data

Thinking

Take your time to absorb all this material. Be willing to read through it several times and ask questions.

Your efforts will be rewarded. In addition to discovering more details about *how* you learn, you'll gain a set of strategies for applying this knowledge to your courses. With these strategies, you can use your knowledge of learning styles to succeed in school.

Above all, aim to recover your natural gift for learning as a master student. Rediscover a world where the boundaries between learning and fun, between work and play, all disappear. While immersing yourself in new experiences, blend the sophistication of an adult with the wonder of a child. This is a path that you can travel for the rest of your life.

Using your Learning Style Profile to SUCCEED

USE THE MODES TO EXPAND YOUR OPTIONS FOR LEARNING

To gain the most benefit from the concept of learning styles, stay flexible. Don't turn your preferred modes into a set of demands or limitations such as: "I can't learn algebra—it's just too abstract." Or, "I can only succeed with instructors who present material in visual terms."

Instead, use the concept of learning *styles* as a path to new learning *strategies*. By developing your skills in all four modes, you can excel in many courses with different kinds of instructors.

USE THE MODES WHILE CHOOSING COURSES

Remember your learning style profile when you're thinking about which classes to take and how to study for each class. If you prefer Mode 1, for example, look for courses that sound interesting and seem worthwhile to you. If you prefer Mode 2, consider classes that center on lectures, reading, and discussion. If you prefer Mode 3, choose courses that include demonstrations, lab sessions, role-playing, and other ways to take action. And if you prefer Mode 4, look for courses that could apply to situations at work, at home, and in your relationships.

ACCEPT CHANGE—AND OCCASIONAL DISCOMFORT

As you seek out chances to develop new modes of learning, keep in mind that discomfort is part of the process. Allow yourself to notice any struggle with a task or lack of interest in completing it. Remember that such feelings are temporary and that you are balancing your learning preferences. By choosing to move through discomfort, you consciously expand your ability to learn in new ways.

USE THE MODES TO EXPLORE YOUR MAJOR

If you enjoy learning in Mode 1, you probably value creativity and human relationships. When choosing a major, consider the arts, English, psychology, or political science.

If Mode 2 is your preference, then you enjoy gathering information and building theories. A major related to math or science might be ideal for you.

If Mode 3 is your favorite, then you like to diagnose problems, arrive at solutions, and use technology. A major related to health care, engineering, or economics could be a logical choice for you.

And if your preference is Mode 4, you probably enjoy taking the initiative, implementing decisions, teaching, managing projects, and moving quickly from planning into action. Consider a major in business or education.

As you prepare to declare a major, remain flexible. Use your knowledge of learning styles to open up possibilities rather than dictate your choices. Also remember that regardless of your preferred mode, you can excel at any job or major; this may just mean developing new skills in other modes.

USE THE MODES OF LEARNING TO EXPLORE YOUR CAREER

Knowing about learning styles becomes especially useful when planning your career.

People who excel at Mode 1 are often skilled at tuning in to the feelings of clients and coworkers. These people can listen with an open mind, tolerate confusion, be sensitive to people's feelings, open up to problems that are difficult to define, and brainstorm a variety of solutions. If you like Mode 1, you may be drawn to a career that centers on human relationships, like counseling or ministry.

People who prefer Mode 2 like to do research and work with ideas. They are skilled at gathering data, interpreting information, and summarizing—arriving at the big picture. Mode 2 learners may work as college teachers, lawyers, technical writers, or journalists.

People who like Mode 3 are drawn to solving problems, making decisions, and checking on progress toward goals. Careers in medicine, engineering, information technology, or another applied science are often ideal for them.

People who enjoy Mode 4 like to influence and lead others. These people are often described as "doers" and "risk takers." Mode 4 learners often excel at managing, negotiating, selling, training, and teaching. They might also work in a leadership role for a nonprofit organization or government agency.

Keep in mind that any career can attract people with a variety of learning styles. For instance, the health care field is large enough to include people who prefer Mode 3 and become family physicians—*and* people who prefer Mode 2 and become medical researchers. ✄

INTENTION STATEMENT

Choosing Success

Success is a choice—your choice. Brainstorm for a few minutes about what you want to achieve after completing your education. Then, create an Intention Statement about a step you can take to choose success, and reach your goals.

To choose success I intend to . . .

SKILLS
snapshot

The Discovery Wheel in the Introduction to this text includes a section labeled Learning Styles. For the next 10 to 15 minutes, go beyond your initial responses to that exercise. Take a snapshot of your skills as they exist today, after reading and doing this chapter.

Begin by reflecting on some recent experiences. Then take another step toward mastery by choosing to follow up on your reflections with a specific action.

Discovery

My score on the Learning Styles section of the Discovery Wheel was . . .

If asked to describe my learning preferences in one sentence, I would say . . .

At the end of this course, I would like my Learning Styles score on the Discovery Wheel to be . . .

Intention

To expand my learning style, I would like to experiment with new strategies for learning, including . . .

One strategy that would have an immediate impact on my success in school is . . .

Action

The new habit that I will adopt in order to use this strategy is . . .

do you have a **MINUTE**?

Take the action statement that you just wrote and translate it into tasks that you can do in 60 seconds or less.

*Don't wait for
that magic time
to come. Make
the time to get the
results in life that
you desire.*

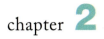

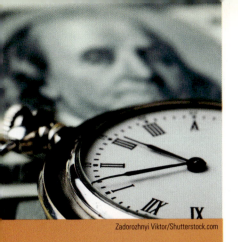

Taking Charge of Your Time & Money

why

Procrastination, lack of planning, and problems with money can quickly undermine your success in school.

how

Take a few minutes to skim this chapter. Find at least three suggestions that look especially useful to you right now. Then write Intention Statements with the specifics about how you will put those ideas into practice.

what if ...

I could meet my goals with time and money to spare?

what is included ...

do you have a minute?

Take a minute to write down an important outcome for today. This is not a to-do list. It is a result that you intend to produce by getting one or more items on your to-do list done. Complete this sentence: Before I go to bed tonight, I want to make absolutely sure that I . . . .

Be here now

Being right here, right now is such a simple idea. It seems obvious. Where else can you be but where you are? When else can you be there but when you are there?

The answer is that you can be somewhere else at any time—in your head. It's common for our thoughts to distract us from where we've chosen to be. Sometimes technology becomes the source of distraction: The arrival of every new text message, Facebook update, or email comes with an attention-grabbing alert. When we let this happen without conscious choice, we lose the benefits of focusing our attention on what's important to us in the present moment.

To "be here now" means to do what you're doing when you're doing it. It means to be where you are when you're there. Students consistently report that focusing attention on the here and now is one of the most powerful tools in this text.

We all have a voice in our head that hardly ever shuts up. If you don't believe it, conduct this experiment: Close your eyes for 10 seconds, and pay attention to what is going on in your head. Please do this right now.

Notice something? Perhaps a voice in your head was saying, "Forget it. I'm in a hurry." Another might have said, "I wonder when 10 seconds is up?" Another could have been saying, "What little voice? I don't hear any little voice."

That's the voice.

This voice can take you anywhere at any time—especially when you are studying. When the voice takes you away, you might appear to be studying, but your brain is somewhere else.

All of us have experienced this voice, as well as the absence of it. When our inner voices are silent, we can experience something that's called "flow": Time no longer seems to exist. We forget worries, aches, pains, reasons, excuses, and justifications. We fully experience the here and now. Life is magic.

Do not expect to be rid of the voice entirely. That is neither possible nor desirable. Inner voices serve a purpose. They enable us to analyze, predict, classify, and understand events out there in the "real" world. The trick is to consciously choose when to be with your inner voice and when to let it go.

Instead of trying to force a stray thought out of your head, simply notice it. Accept it. Tell yourself, "There's that thought again." Then gently return your attention to the task at hand. That thought, or another, will come back. Your mind will drift. Simply notice again where your thoughts take you, and gently bring yourself back to the here and now.

Also remember that planning supports this Power Process. Goals are tools that we create to guide our action in the present. Time-management techniques—calendars, lists, and all the rest—have only one purpose. They reveal what's most important for you to focus on right *now*. Ironically, one way to create flow experiences is to plan for them.

The idea behind this Power Process is simple. When you listen to a lecture, listen to a lecture. When you read this text, read this text. And when you choose to daydream, daydream. Do what you're doing when you're doing it. Be where you are when you're there.

Be here now . . . and now . . . and now. ▰

ko/Shutterstock.com

© 2019 Cengage Learning, Inc. May not be scanned, copied or duplicated, or posted to a publicly accessible website, in whole or in part.

You've got the time—
AND THE MONEY

When you say you don't have enough time or money, you might really be saying that you are not spending what you do have in the way that you want.

The words time management *may call forth images of restriction and control.* You might visualize a prune-faced Scrooge hunched over your shoulder, stopwatch in hand, telling you what to do every minute. Bad news.

The good news is you do have enough time for the things you want to accomplish in life. All it takes is thinking about the possibilities and making conscious choices.

Time is an equal opportunity resource. All of us, regardless of gender, race, creed, or national origin, have exactly the same number of hours in a week. No matter how famous we are, no matter how rich or poor, we all get 168 hours to spend each week—no more, no less.

Time is also an unusual commodity. It cannot be saved. You can't stockpile time like wood for the stove or food for the winter. It can't be seen, heard, touched, tasted, or smelled.

Time is a nonrenewable resource. If you're out of wood, you can chop some more. If you're out of money, you can earn a little extra. If you're out of love, there is still hope. If you're out of health, it can often be restored. But when you're out of time, that's it. When this minute is gone, it's gone.

Sometimes it seems that your friends control your time; your boss controls your time; your teachers or your parents or your kids or somebody else controls your time. Maybe that is not true, though.

Approach time as if you are in control. When you say you don't have enough time, you might really be saying that you are not spending the time you *do* have in the way that you want. This chapter is about ways to solve that problem.

In addition, look for the **Do you have a minute?** boxes throughout this text. These suggest ways for you to make progress toward your goals by completing a task that takes about 60 seconds.

Also approach money as if you are in control. When you say you don't have enough money, the real issue might be that you are not spending the money you *do* have in ways that align with your values.

Most money problems result from spending more than is available. It's that simple, even though we often do everything we can to make the problem much more complicated. The solution also is simple: Don't spend more than you have. If you are spending more than you have, then increase your income, decrease your spending, or do both.

The point is that you are in control of what you earn and spend. This idea has never won a Nobel Prize in Economics, but you won't go broke applying it.

Everything written about time and money management can be reduced to three main ideas:

1. **Know exactly *what* you want.** State your wants as clear, specific goals. And put them in writing.

When our lives lack this quality, we spend most of our time responding to interruptions, last-minute projects, and emergencies. Life feels like a scramble to just survive. We're so busy achieving someone else's goals that we forget about getting what *we* want.

2. **Know *how* to get what you want.** Take action to meet your goals, including financial goals. Determine what you'll do *today* to get what you want in the future. Put those actions in writing as well.

3. **Take action to *get* what you want.** When schedules get tight, we often drop important activities such as exercising and fixing nutritious meals. We postpone them for that elusive day when we'll finally "have the time" or "have the money."

Don't wait for that magic time to come. *Make* the time to get the results in life that you desire. Use the suggestions and exercises in this chapter to empower yourself.

The most useful strategies for managing time and money are not new. These strategies are all based on the cycle of discovery, intention, and action that you're already using in this text. Throw in the ability to add and subtract, and you have everything you need to manage your time and your money. Spend these valuable resources in ways that align with your values. ◢

Setting and achieving
GOALS

Many people have no goals or have only vague, idealized notions of what they want. They are wonderful, fuzzy, safe thoughts such as "I want to be a good person," "I want to be financially secure," or "I want to be happy."

General outcomes such as these have potential as achievable goals. When we *keep* these goals in a general form, however, we may become confused about ways to actually achieve them.

Make your goal as real as a finely tuned engine. There is nothing vague or fuzzy about engines. You can see them, feel them, and hear them. You can take them apart and inspect the moving parts.

Goals can be every bit as real and useful. If you really want to meet a goal, then take it apart. Inspect the moving parts—the physical actions that you will take to make the goal happen and fine-tune your life.

Some presentations about goal setting make the whole process seem like a painful exercise in self-discipline. Don't believe it. Setting and achieving goals is really about having fun for the long run. It's about getting what you want in the future and enjoying every step along the way.

Write down your goals. Writing down your goals greatly increases your chances of meeting them. Writing exposes undefined terms, unrealistic time frames, and other symptoms of fuzzy thinking.

If you've been completing Intention Statements as explained in the Introduction to this text, then you've already had experience writing goals. Both goals and Intention Statements address changes you want to make in your behavior, your values, your circumstances—or all of these.

Write specific goals. State your goals in writing as observable outcomes or measurable results. Think in detail about how things will be different once your goals are attained. List the changes in what you'll see, feel, touch, taste, hear, be, do, or have.

Suppose that one of your goals is to become a better student by studying harder. You're headed in a powerful direction; now translate that goal into a concrete action, such as "I will study two hours for every hour I'm in class."

Specific goals make clear what actions are needed or what results are expected. Consider these examples:

Vague Goal	Specific Goal
Get a good education	Graduate with BS degree in engineering, with honors, by 2021
Get good grades	Earn a 3.5 grade point average next semester
Enhance my spiritual life	Join a church in my neighborhood with a strong tradition of community service
Improve my appearance	Lose 6 pounds during the next 6 months
Get control of my money	Have $5,000 in my savings account by July 1 of next year

Write goals in several time frames. To get a comprehensive vision of your future, write down the following:

- **Long-term goals.** Long-term goals represent major targets in your life. These goals can take 5 to 20 years to achieve. In some cases, they will take a lifetime. They can include goals in education, careers, personal relationships, travel, financial security—whatever is important to you. Consider the answers to the following questions as you create your long-term goals: What do you want to accomplish in your life? Do you want your life to make a statement? If so, what is that statement?

- **Midterm goals.** Midterm goals are objectives you can accomplish in one to five years. They include goals such as completing a course of education, paying off a car loan, or achieving a specific career level. These goals usually support your long-term goals.

- **Short-term goals.** Short-term goals are the ones you can accomplish in a year or less. These goals are specific achievements, such as completing a particular course or group of courses, hiking down the Appalachian Trail, or organizing a family reunion. A short-term financial goal would probably include an exact dollar amount. Whatever your short-term goals are, they will require action now or in the near future.

Write goals in several areas of life. People who set goals in only one area of life—such as their career—may find that their personal growth becomes one-sided. They might experience success at work while neglecting their health or relationships with family members and friends. To avoid this outcome, set goals in a variety of categories such as:

- Education
- Career
- Health
- Wealth
- Family life
- Friendships
- Volunteering and community service
- Spirituality

Put habits in place to meet your goals. Much of your behavior is habitual. Take advantage of this fact to meet your goals. After setting a goal, choose at least one habit that you will adopt to achieve it. For example:

- If your goal is to lose 10 pounds this year, then make it a habit to replace dessert with a serving of fruit.
- If your goal is to pay off your credit card debt, then make it a habit to pay more than the minimum amount due each month.
- If your goal is to write a book that will promote your business, then make it a habit to write for 30 minutes every day.

Translating goals into habits gives you a game that you can win. The pay-off for a long-term goal might not come for years. A habit is something that you can do today and reward yourself for in the present. Goals give you a direction. Habits give you a *system* for making daily progress. The goals that lead to changes in your daily behavior are the goals that you're most likely to achieve.

To succeed at habit change, start small. Instead of planning to do yoga for one hour every day, make it your intention to simply step on a yoga mat as soon as you wake up. Instead of planning to read 50 books this year, make it your intention to simply read one page every night before you go to bed. When your habits involve small behaviors, you're more likely to do them even when you don't feel motivated. Once you put a small behavior change in place, it can naturally expand over time.

Also link each habit to a cue that will remind you to do the behavior. For example:

- After starting the microwave (cue), do one push up (behavior).

- After putting on your pajamas (cue), lay out the clothes you will wear to exercise in the morning (behavior).
- After you get home from school (cue), fill a glass with water and put it in your study area (behavior).
- After you enter the grocery store (cue), pick out one new vegetable to eat (behavior).
- After you get out of bed in the morning (cue), take one deep breath (behavior).
- After using the bathroom (cue), step on to a yoga mat and do one simple stretch (behavior).

Finally, remember to celebrate every time that you practice a new habit. This can be as simple as saying *Yes!* or *Way to go!* to yourself. Savor every success, no matter how small. Then enjoy the results as they unfold in your life.

Reflect on your goals. Each week, take a few minutes to think about your goals. You can perform the following spot checks:

- ***Check in with your feelings.*** Think about how the process of setting your goals felt. Consider the satisfaction you'll gain in attaining your objectives. If you don't feel a significant emotional connection with a written goal, consider letting it go or filing it away to review later.
- ***Check for alignment.*** Look for connections among your goals. Do your short-term goals align with your midterm goals? Will your midterm goals help you achieve your long-term goals? Look for a fit between all of your goals and your purpose for taking part in higher education as well as your overall purpose in life.
- ***Check for obstacles.*** All kinds of things can come between you and your goals, such as constraints on time and money. Anticipate obstacles and start looking now for workable solutions.
- ***Check for next steps.*** Decide on a list of small, achievable steps you can take right away to accomplish each of your short-term goals. Write these small steps down on a calendar (to schedule them for a specific day) or on a to-do list.

Move into action immediately. The idea of making New Year's resolutions is the butt of countless jokes. On January 1, we swear to start exercising regularly. By February 1, we're reaching for the TV remote instead of the jogging shoes.

Don't let your goals suffer such a fate. To increase your odds of success, take immediate action. Decrease the gap between stating a goal and starting to achieve it. If you slip up and forget about your goal, you can get back on track at any time by *doing* something about it. Make those jokes about resolutions a part of your past, not a predictor of your future. ✖

Time management
ESSENTIALS

Think back to the simpler times of your life. During your early school years, you went to class at regular hours. Then you had plenty of time to play. Later you learned to make time for homework. During high school you probably added some extracurricular activities. Even so, your teachers guided your schedule, gave you regular assignments, and reminded you about them.

In higher education, all of this changes. You're now juggling multiple courses and assignments—and perhaps a job and family as well. Compared to high school teachers, your current instructors are "hands-off." They give assignments and simply expect you to get them done. No one is looking over your shoulder to manage your schedule. No one checks on your progress. It's all up to you.

This is something that many students in higher education forget. They approach college-level work with the mindset of a high-school student.

To succeed in school and the workplace, develop time management skills for the twenty-first century. Following are some essential tools and habits.

YOUR CALENDAR

If you don't already have this essential tool, get one today. Use a calendar to remind yourself about commitments that will take place on a specific date, a specific time, or both. Examples are classes, tests, meetings, appointments, and work hours. You can also schedule due dates for assignments, review sessions, study group meetings, social gatherings, and any other important event.

Many students use a paper-based calendar that they carry along with

their textbooks and class notes. Other people favor online calendars. Calendar apps for desktop computers and mobile devices are also popular. Check out the options. Then settle on one that you will actually use every day.

People who are new to higher education often struggle with their lack of structured time. Aside from class meetings, there is no fixed "work day" for students. As a result, some treat all nonclass time as "free time" and focus on having fun or working. These students put their education at risk.

Other students go to the opposite extreme and treat every waking hour as study time. They risk burnout.

You can avoid both mistakes by using your calendar. Schedule three kinds of events:

- **Fixed commitments.** Include class time, work time, and other events that are determined in advance.
- **Study sessions.** Over the course of a full week, see if you can schedule two hours of study time for every hour that you spend in class. Avoid scheduling marathon study sessions, however. Plan for shorter sessions. Three 2-hour sessions are usually far more productive than one 6-hour session.
- **Time for other tasks.** See if you can find an hour each day to do items on your to-do list (explained in the next section).

This approach to scheduling will quickly reveal whether you have too many commitments. Keep adjusting your schedule until you create one that supports your success. Remember that success means having some

unscheduled time on most days to deal with surprises—and just relax.

YOUR PROJECT LIST AND TO-DO LIST

It's not wise—or even possible—to schedule everything you want to do. For important items that do *not* have to be done on a certain date or time, create lists.

Two time-tested tools for creating lists are pen and paper. Set aside a specific notebook for your lists. Or, write each list item on a separate 3×5 card. You can also create lists with apps for computers and mobile devices. As with your calendar, choose tools that you will use daily.

After you settle on a list manager, create two lists. The first is a project list. A *project* is any goal that:

- You want to achieve during this term.
- Requires more than one action.

Projects include papers to write, presentations to prepare, and other multistep class assignments. Projects can also include goals that go beyond school. For example, do you want to set up a personal website? That's a project. Do you want to write a career plan or find a romantic partner? Those are projects, too.

Take the time to write a complete project list. With this list and your calendar, you get the "big picture" of your life—an overview of all of your current commitments. This perspective is essential for effective time management.

The second list is a to-do list. This includes the specific actions you'll take to get your projects done. Examples are phone calls to make, e-mails to send, and errands to run.

As you finish each to-do item, delete it from your list. Savor the resulting sense of accomplishment. Also add new to-do items as you think of them.

YOUR IN-BASKETS

Consider all the "inputs" you get during a typical day—e-mails, text messages, phone calls, "snail mail," and other papers. Many of these call for follow-up action on your part.

Collect all of this stuff with in-baskets. Then you can process each item, one at a time, and not worry that you're forgetting something.

You will use several in-baskets. Start with a tray or folder for loose papers. Also, create a folder on your computer desktop for e-mail attachments and other digital documents. In addition, think of your e-mail software as another in-basket.

Suppose you get an idea during the day that you want to capture, but you don't have time to process it right away. Just jot it down on a piece of paper and throw it in your in-basket. Or, use any app on your smartphone that allows you to quickly create notes or voice memos. This app is now another in-basket for you.

YOUR REVIEW SESSIONS

With your calendar, lists, and in-baskets, you have the core tools for time management. Now develop the habit of reviewing their contents on a regular basis.

The daily review. Once each day, check your calendar and to-do list. This is your guide to what to complete within the next 24 hours.

The weekly review. Schedule a regular time—such as Friday afternoon or Sunday night—for a weekly review. Begin by taking the items from your in-baskets and clarifying what to do about them. For each item, you have three basic options:

- *Delete it.* Trash it or toss it in a recycling bin.
- *Do it now.* This works well for tasks such as making a quick phone call.
- *Defer it.* That is, write a reminder to handle it later. This reminder goes on your calendar, project list, or to-do list.

Because each item in the above list starts with a *D*, this is called the "three-D" method of cleaning out your in-baskets.

Some of the things that you collect will not require any follow-up action. Even so, you might want to keep them on hand so that you can find them later. These are reference items such as insurance policies, owner's manuals, and contact information for your friends and family members.

Set up simple filing systems for reference items. Use file folders for pieces of paper. Give each folder a name, and store the folders in alphabetical order. On your computer, create folders for each of your current classes and projects.

Set a goal to empty all your in-baskets once per week with the three-D method. This is an exercise in critical thinking, and it takes time. The reward is clarity and peace of mind.

Also make time during the weekly review to update your other time management tools. Check your calendar for scheduled events. Make sure your project list is accurate. Also focus on your to-do list: Does it include all the actions you'll need to do this week to complete your projects on time? If not, revise the list.

The end-of-term review. At the end of each quarter or semester, schedule an hour to reflect on your life as a whole. Ask yourself:

- Am I making time for things that are important as well as urgent?
- Am I making progress on my long-term goals?
- Are my goals and daily activities truly aligned with my core values?

Your answers to these questions can lead to new goals, schedules, projects, and to-do items. What's truly essential about time management is the opportunity to keep creating the life of your dreams. ✦

do you have a
MINUTE?

Take a minute to take action on one suggestion from this article. For example:

- Choose a paper-based calendar or calendar app that you'll use daily.
- Choose a tool to manage lists. Notebooks, index cards, and apps are all options. Test them to find the best fit for you.
- Use the one-minute rule to empty your in-basket: If you can respond to an item in 60 seconds or less, just do it now.

Procrastination
UNPLUGGED

The terms *self-discipline*, *willpower*, and *motivation* are often used to describe something missing in ourselves. Time after time, we invoke these words to explain another person's success—or our own shortcomings: "If I were more motivated, I'd get more involved in school." "Of course she got an A. She has self-discipline." "If I had more willpower, I'd lose weight."

It seems that certain people are born with lots of motivation, whereas others miss out on it.

An alternative way of thinking is to stop assuming that motivation is mysterious, determined at birth, or hard to come by. In fact, perhaps the whole concept of motivation is just a myth. Maybe what we call motivation is something that you already possess—the ability to do a task even when you don't feel like it.

We don't need the concept of motivation to change our behavior. Rather, immediate action can flow from genuine commitment. With that idea in mind, test the following suggestions.

CHECK FOR ATTITUDES THAT PROMOTE PROCRASTINATION

Certain attitudes fuel procrastination and keep you from experiencing the rewards in life that you deserve. In their book *Procrastination: Why You Do It and What to Do About It*, psychologists Jane Burka and Lenora Yuen list these examples:

- I must be perfect.
- Everything I do should go easily and without effort.
- It's safer to do nothing than to take a risk and fail.
- If it's not done right, it's not worth doing at all.
- If I do well this time, I must always do well.
- If I succeed, someone will get hurt.[1]

If you find such beliefs running through your mind, write them down. Getting a belief out of your head and onto paper can rob that belief of its power. Also write a more effective belief that you want to adopt. For example: "Even if I don't complete this task perfectly, it's good enough for now, and I can still learn from my mistakes."

ACCEPT YOUR FEELINGS OF RESISTANCE— THEN TAKE ACTION

If you wait to exercise until you feel energetic, you might wait for months. Instead, get moving now and watch your feelings change. After five minutes of brisk walking, you might be in the mood for a 20-minute run. Don't wait to feel "motivated"

before you take action. Instead, apply the principle that action *creates* motivation.

This principle can be applied to any task you've been putting off. You can move into action no matter how you feel about a task. Simply notice your feelings of resistance, accept them, and then do one small task related to your goal. Then do one more task, and another. Keep at it, one task at a time, and watch procrastination disappear. ✂

do you have a MINUTE?

Choose a project that you've been putting off. Take one minute to define the very next action you'll take to get this project done.

Put an end to
MONEY WORRIES

If you want to end money worries, then clarify your intentions to earn more and spend less. Following are ideas you can use immediately.

EARN MORE

Get financial aid. Student grants, scholarships, and low-interest loans can play a major role in your college success by freeing you up from having to work full-time or even part-time. Many students assume they don't qualify for financial aid. That assumption could cost you thousands of dollars. Visit the financial aid office at your school to discover your options.

Work at a job while you're in school. If you work while you're in school, you earn more than money. You gain experience, establish references, interact with a variety of people, and make contact with people who might hire you in the future. Also, regular income in any amount can make a difference to your monthly cash flow.

Many students work full-time or part-time jobs. Work and school don't have to conflict, especially if you plan your week carefully and ask for your employer's support.

On most campuses, the financial aid office employs a person whose job it is to help students find work while they're in school. Find that person.

See whether you can find a job related to your chosen career. Even an entry-level job in your field can provide valuable experience. Once you've been in such a job for a while, find out how to get promoted.

Ask for a raise. Find out the salary range for the job you have or want. With this information in mind, you'll be able to tell whether a job interviewer or supervisor is offering a salary that's unreasonably low.

When the topic of salary comes up, the person on the other side of the desk will probably start by asking a question: *What figure did you have in mind?*

This is a tricky question. Naming a figure that's too high could get you screened out. Naming a figure that's too low could undermine your credibility and lock you into in a smaller paycheck for a long time. Instead of naming a figure at this point, say something like: *I am open to discussion. What range from low to high do you have in mind?*

The other person's first answer is likely to be in the lower end of the range that they're prepared to offer. If their figure is within your desired range, then say: *I think we're close. What would it take to get to . . . ?* End the sentence with a number that's toward the high end of your desired range. This gives you room to negotiate.

Start a business on the side.
Consider a service you could offer on a part-time basis—anything from lawn mowing to computer consulting. Students can boost their income in many other ways, such as running errands, giving guitar lessons, tutoring, designing websites, walking pets, detailing cars, and house sitting. Charge reasonable rates, provide impeccable service, and ask your clients for referrals. Earning even a couple of hundred more dollars each month can make a difference in your experience of money.

Think hard about what your potential customers or clients want. What problems do they want to solve? What benefits do they want to experience? Offer your product or service as an answer.

Be a high performer. Once you get a job or start a business, make it your intention to excel at what you do. Make yourself indispensable. Look for ways to excel at your job by building relationships, becoming a rock-star collaborator, and consistently delivering results. Suggest ideas that can increase revenue, decrease costs, solve problems, and make processes more efficient. Then ask to get assigned to the teams that implement your ideas.

Be a lifetime learner. You can use your education to develop knowledge, experience, and skills that create income for the rest of your life. Once you graduate and land a job in your chosen field, continue your education. Look for ways to gain additional skills or certifications that lead to more fulfilling work assignments—and more money in the future.

SPEND LESS

Look to big-ticket items. When you look for places to cut expenses, start with the items that cost the most. Choices about where to live, for example, can save you thousands of dollars. Sometimes a place a little farther from campus, or a smaller house or apartment, will be much less expensive. You can also keep your housing costs down by finding a roommate. Offer to do repairs or maintenance in exchange for reduced rent. Pay your rent on time, and treat property with respect.

Another high-ticket item is a car. Take the cost of buying or leasing and then add expenses for parking, insurance, repairs, gas, maintenance, and tires. You might find that it makes more sense to walk, bike, use public transportation, ride a campus shuttle, and call for an occasional taxi ride. Or carpool. Find friends with a car, and chip in for gas.

Track your expenses to discover the main drains on your finances. Then focus on one or two areas where you can reduce spending while continuing to pay your fixed monthly bills such as rent and tuition.

Save money on eating and drinking.

This single suggestion could significantly lower your expenses. Instead of hitting a restaurant or bar, head to the grocery store.

Cooking for yourself doesn't need to take much time if you do a little menu planning. Create a list of your five favorite home-cooked meals. Learn how to prepare them. Then keep ingredients for these meals always on hand. To reduce grocery bills, buy these ingredients in bulk.

If you live in a dorm, review the different meal plans you can buy. Some schools offer meal plans for students who live off campus. These plans might be cheaper than eating in restaurants while you're on campus.

Lower your phone bills.

If you use a cell phone, pull out a copy of your latest bill. Review how many minutes you used last month. Perhaps you could get by with a less expensive phone, fewer minutes, fewer text messages, and a cheaper plan.

Do an Internet search on *cell phone plan comparison,* and see whether you could save money by switching providers. Also consider a family calling plan, which might cost less than a separate plan for each person. In addition, consider whether you need a home phone (a landline) *and* a cell phone. Dropping the home phone could save you money right away.

Pay cash.

To avoid interest charges, deal in cash. If you don't have the cash, don't buy. Buying on credit makes it more difficult to monitor spending. You can easily bust next month's money plan with this month's credit card purchases.

Postpone purchases.

If you plan to buy something, leave your checkbook or credit card at home when you first go shopping. Look at all the possibilities. Then go home and make your decision when you don't feel pressured. When you are ready to buy, wait a week, even if the salesperson pressures you. What seems like a necessity today may not even cross your mind the day after tomorrow.

Notice what you spend on "fun."

Blowing your money on fun is fun. It is also a fast way to blow your savings. When you spend money on entertainment, ask yourself what the benefits will be and whether you could get the same benefits for less money.

Use the envelope system.

After reviewing your monthly income and expenses, put a certain amount of cash each week in an envelope labeled *Entertainment/Eating Out.* When the envelope is empty, stop spending money on these items for the rest of the week. If you use online banking, see whether you can create separate accounts for various spending categories. Then deposit a fixed amount of money into each of those accounts. This is an electronic version of the envelope system.

Don't compete with big spenders.

When you watch other people spend their money, remember that you don't know the whole story. Some students have parents with deep pockets. Others head to Mexico every year for spring break but finance the trips with high-interest credit cards. If you find yourself feeling pressured to spend money so that you can keep up with other people, stop to think about how much it will cost over the long run. Maybe it's time to shop around for some new friends. ✄

INTENTION STATEMENT

journal entry **3**

Show me the money

See whether you can use *The Essential Guide to Becoming a Master Student* to create a financial gain that is many times more than the cost of the book. Scan the entire text, and look for suggestions that you can turn into Intention Statements that could help you save money or increase income. For example, you might use suggestions for career planning to find your next job more quickly—and start earning money sooner. Write down the ideas that you find, and then write at least two intentions.

I intend to . . .

I intend to . . .

Use credit
WITH CARE

A good credit rating will serve you for a lifetime. With this asset, you'll be able to borrow money any time you need it. A poor credit rating, however, can keep you from getting a car or a house in the future. You might also have to pay higher insurance rates, and you could even be turned down for a job.

To take charge of your credit, borrow money only when truly necessary. If you do borrow, then make all of your payments, and make them on time. This is especially important for managing credit cards and student loans.

USE CREDIT CARDS WITH CAUTION

Pay off the balance each month. An unpaid credit card balance is a sure sign that you are spending more money than you have. To avoid this outcome, keep track of how much you spend with credit cards each month. Set a goal to pay off the entire card balance each month, on time, to avoid finance or late charges.

Scrutinize credit card offers. Finding a card with a lower interest rate can make a dramatic difference. However, look carefully at credit card offers. Low rates may be temporary. After a few months, they could double or even triple. Also look for annual fees, late fees, and other charges buried in the fine print.

Avoid cash advances. Due to their high interest rates and fees, credit cards are not a great source of spare cash. Even when you get cash advances on these cards from an ATM, it's still borrowed money. As an alternative, get a debit card tied to a checking account. Use that card when you need cash on the go.

Check statements against your records. File your credit card receipts each month. When you get the bill for each card, check it against your receipts for accuracy. Mistakes in billing are rare, but they can happen. In addition, checking your statement reveals the interest rate and fees that are being applied to your account.

Use just one credit card. To simplify your financial life and take charge of your credit, consider using only one card. Choose one with no annual fee and the lowest interest rate. Consider the bottom line, and be selective. If you do have more than one credit card, pay off the one with the highest interest rate first. Then consider canceling that card.

MANAGE STUDENT LOANS

Choose schools with costs in mind. If you decide to transfer to another school, you can save thousands of dollars the moment you sign your application for admission. In addition to choosing schools on the basis of reputation, consider how much they cost and the financial aid packages that they offer.

Avoid debt when possible. The surest way to manage debt is to avoid it altogether. If you do take out loans, borrow only the amount that you cannot get from other sources—scholarships, grants, employment, gifts from relatives, and personal savings. Predict what your income will be when the first loan payments are due, and whether you'll make enough money to manage continuing payments.

Also set a target date for graduation, and stick to it. The fewer years you go to school, the lower your debt.

Shop carefully for loans. Go to the financial aid office and ask whether you can get a Stafford loan. These are fixed-rate, low-interest loans from the federal government. For more information on the loans that are available to you, visit **www.studentaid.ed.gov**.

If your parents are helping to pay for your education, they can apply for a PLUS loan. There is no income limit, and parents can borrow up to the total cost of their children's education.

If at all possible, avoid loans from privately owned companies. These companies often charge higher interest rates and impose terms that are less favorable to students. While you're shopping around, ask about options for repaying your loans. Lenders might allow you to extend the payments over a longer period or adjust the amount of your monthly payment based on your income. ✄

do you have a MINUTE?

Search your school's website for the location, phone number, and e-mail address of the financial aid office.

Take a snapshot of your current skills at working with time and money. Also think about the next step you'll take to develop more mastery in these areas of your life.

Discovery

My score on the Time and Money section of the Discovery Wheel was . . .

After reading this chapter and experimenting with some of the suggestions, I would describe my ability to set and achieve goals as . . .

I would describe my ability to manage money as . . .

Intention

When it comes to managing time more effectively, the most important change for me to make right now is . . .

When it comes to managing money more effectively, the most important change for me to make right now is . . .

Action

To make the changes that I just described, the new habits that I will adopt are . . .

At the end of this course, I would like my Time and Money score on the Discovery Wheel to be . . .

do you have a MINUTE?

Take one minute to go online to research other time management strategies. One option is to start with the Pomodoro Technique, where you set a timer for 25 minutes and focus on one task for the whole time. Learn more at http://pomodorotechnique.com.

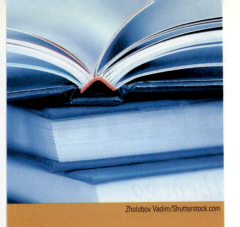

why

Higher education requires extensive reading of complex material.

how

Recall a time when you encountered problems with reading, such as finding words you didn't understand or pausing to reread paragraphs more than once. Then identify at least three specific reading skills you want to gain from this chapter.

what if...

I could finish my reading with time to spare and easily recall the key points?

Achieving Your Purpose for Reading

what is included ...

do you have a minute?

Find a tool for building your vocabulary. For example, test your web browser to see if it will display definitions when you control-click on a word. You could also search for a dictionary app and download it to your mobile phone or tablet.

PHASE 1: *Before you read*

STEP 1: PREVIEW

Before you start reading, preview the entire assignment. You don't have to memorize what you preview to get value from this step. Previewing sets the stage for incoming information by warming up a space in your mental storage area.

If you are starting a new book, look over the table of contents, and flip through the text page by page. If you're going to read one chapter, flip through the pages of that chapter. Even if your assignment is merely a few pages in a book, you can benefit from a brief preview of the table of contents.

Read all chapter headings and subheadings. Like the headlines in a newspaper, these are usually printed in large, bold type. Often headings are brief summaries in themselves.

Keep an eye out for summary statements. If the assignment is long or complex, read the summary first. Many textbooks have summaries in the introduction or at the end of each chapter.

When previewing, seek out familiar concepts, facts, or ideas. These items can help increase comprehension by linking new information to previously learned material. Take a few moments to reflect on what you already know about the subject—even if you think you know nothing. This technique prepares your brain to accept new information.

Look for ideas that spark your imagination or curiosity. Inspect diagrams, charts, tables, graphs, and photographs.

Imagine what kinds of questions will show up on a test. Previewing helps to clarify your purpose for reading. Ask yourself what you will do with this material and how it can relate to your long-term goals. Will you be reading just to get the main points? Key supporting details? Additional

The magic of metacognition

It's pronounced "metta-cog-ni-shun." *Meta* means "beyond" or "above." *Cognition* refers to everything that goes on inside your brain—perceiving, thinking, learning. Metacognition is thinking *about* thinking, learning *about* learning. It's your ability to stand "above" your mental processes—to observe them and to take conscious control of them. Metacognition is one of the main benefits of higher education.

The key is to stop periodically and reflect on how well you're actually mastering a concept or skill.

The challenge is that we can easily believe that we're learning when we're actually not.

This becomes a problem when students rely too much on strategies such as underlining, highlighting, and passively rereading a text. The fact that you can recognize or repeat concepts from your texts or notes does not mean that you can explain those concepts in your own words or use them to solve problems.

To get the most from your reading and notes, practice metacognition to assess your progress. After reading a chapter in a textbook or reviewing a section of your class notes, take a few minutes to check for understanding. You can do this by:

- Stating how new concepts relate to something that you already know.
- Making up questions about what you've just read and writing brief answers to them.
- Drawing pictures, charts, or diagrams that express concepts in visual terms.
- Explaining what you've just read to other people and asking them if your explanation is clear.
- Listing the actions that you would take to put a concept into practice.
- Listing the underlying principles or "rules" for solving a problem or performing a task.
- Asking yourself if you're confused by anything you've just read and listing questions that you intend to ask in class.

With strategies such as these, you change from a passive consumer of information into an active learner on a path to mastery. The magic of metacognition is that you become your own best teacher.

details? All of the above? Your answers will guide what you do with each step that follows.

Keep your preview short. If the entire reading assignment will take less than an hour, your preview might take five minutes. Previewing is also a way to get yourself started when an assignment looks too big to handle. It is an easy way to step into the material.

STEP 2: OUTLINE

With complex material, take time to understand the structure of what you are about to read. Outlining actively organizes your thoughts about the assignment and can help make complex information easier to understand.

If your textbook provides chapter outlines, spend some time studying them. When an outline is not provided, sketch a brief one in the margin of your book or at the beginning of your notes on a separate sheet of paper. Later, as you read and take notes, you can add to your outline.

Headings in the text can serve as major and minor entries in your outline. For example, the heading for this article is "Phase 1: Before you read," and the subheadings list the three steps in this phase. When you outline, feel free to rewrite headings so that they are more meaningful to you.

The amount of time you spend on this outlining step will vary. For some assignments, a 10-second mental outline is all you might need. For other assignments (fiction and poetry, for example), you can skip this step altogether.

STEP 3: QUESTION

Before you begin a careful reading, determine what you want from the assignment. Then write down a list of questions, including any questions that resulted from your preview of the materials.

Another useful technique is to turn chapter headings and subheadings into questions. For example, if a heading is "Transference and Suggestion," you can ask yourself, "What are *transference* and *suggestion*? How does *transference* relate to *suggestion*?" Make up a quiz as if you were teaching this subject to your classmates.

If there are no headings, look for key sentences and turn them into questions. These sentences usually show up at the beginnings or ends of paragraphs and sections.

The purpose of making up questions is to wake up your brain. Answer the main questions in your mind *before* you read the text. Then compare your initial answers to the author's. If you're reading for a math course, see if you can solve sample problems *before* you find the solution in the text. Take your unanswered questions and unsolved problems to class, where they can be springboards for class discussion.

Demand your money's worth from your textbook. If you do not understand a concept, write specific questions about it. The more detailed your questions, the more powerful this technique becomes. ✄

PHASE 2: *While you read*

STEP 4: FOCUS

You have previewed the reading assignment, organized it in your mind or on paper, and formulated questions. Now you are ready to begin reading.

It's easy to fool yourself about reading. Just having an open book in your hand and moving your eyes across a page doesn't mean that you are reading effectively. Reading takes mental focus.

As you read, be conscious of where you are and what you are doing. Use the "Power Process: Be here now."

When you notice your attention wandering, gently bring it back to the present moment. There are many ways to do this.

To begin, get in a position to stay focused. If you observe chief executive officers, you'll find that some of them wear out the front of their chair first. They're literally on the edge of their seat. Approach your reading assignment in the same way. Sit up. Keep your spine straight. Avoid reading in bed, except for fun.

Avoid marathon reading sessions. Schedule breaks and set a reasonable goal for the entire session. Then reward yourself with an enjoyable activity for 10 or 15 minutes every hour or two.

For difficult reading, set more limited goals. Read for a half hour and then take a break. Most students find that shorter periods of reading distributed throughout the day and week can be more effective than long sessions.

Visualize the material. Form mental pictures of the concepts as they are presented. If you read that a voucher system can help control cash disbursements, picture a voucher handing out dollar bills. Using visual imagery in this way can help deepen your understanding of the text while allowing information to be transferred into your long-term memory.

Read material out loud, especially if it is complicated. Some of us remember better and understand more quickly when we hear an idea.

Get a "feel" for the subject. For example, let's say you are reading about a microorganism—a paramecium—in your biology text. Imagine what it would feel like to run your finger around the long, cigar-shaped body of the organism. Imagine feeling the large fold of its gullet on one side and the tickle of the hairy little cilia as they wiggle in your hand.

In addition, predict how the author will answer your key questions. Then read to find out if your predictions were accurate.

STEP 5: FLAG ANSWERS

As you read, seek out the answers to your questions. You are a detective, watching for every clue. When you do find an answer, flag it so that it stands out on the page.

Deface your books. Have fun. Flag answers by highlighting, underlining, writing comments, filling in your outline, or marking up pages in any other way that helps you. Indulge yourself as you never could with your grade school books.

Marking up your books offers other benefits. When you read with a highlighter, pen, or pencil in your hand, you involve your kinesthetic senses of touch and motion. This can help build strong neural pathways in your memory.

You can mark up a text in many ways. For example:

- Place an asterisk (*) or an exclamation point (!) next to an especially important sentence or term.
- Circle key terms and words to look up later in a dictionary.
- Write short definitions of key terms in the margin.
- Write a *Q* in the margin to highlight possible test questions, passages you don't understand, and questions to ask in class.
- Write personal comments in the margin—points of agreement or disagreement with the author.
- Write mini-indexes in the margin—that is, the other pages in the book where the same topic is discussed.
- Write summaries in your own words.
- Rewrite chapter titles, headings, and subheadings so that they're more meaningful to you.
- Draw diagrams, pictures, tables, or maps to translate text into visuals.
- Number each step in a list or series of related points.

- In the margins, write notes about the relationships between elements in your reading. For instance, note connections between an idea and examples of that idea.
- If you infer an answer to a question or come up with another idea of your own, write that down too.

Avoid marking up a text too soon. Wait until you complete a chapter or section to make sure you know the key points. Then mark up the text. Sometimes, flagging answers after you read each paragraph works best.

Also remember that the purpose of making marks in a text is to call out important concepts that you will use to create questions and quiz yourself later. Flagging key information can save lots of time when you are studying for tests. With this in mind, highlight or underline sparingly—usually less than 10 percent of the text. If you mark up too much on a page, you defeat the purpose: to flag the most important material for review.

Finally, note when you don't find the answers you are looking for. Ask these questions in class, or see your instructor personally. Demand that your textbooks give you what you want—answers. ✄

Muscle Reading—a leaner approach

Keep in mind that Muscle Reading is an overall approach, not a rigid, step-by-step procedure. Here's a shorter variation that students have found helpful. Practice it with any chapter in this text:

- **Preview and question.** Flip through the pages, looking at anything that catches your eye—headings, subheadings, illustrations, photographs. Turn the title of each article into a question. List your questions on a separate sheet of paper, or write each question on a 3 × 5 card.
- **Read to answer your questions.** Read each article. Then go back over the text and underline or highlight direct answers to the appropriate questions on your list.
- **Recite and review.** When you're done with the chapter, close the text. Recite by reading each question—and answering it—out loud. Review the chapter by looking up the answers to your questions. (It's easy—they're already highlighted.) Review again by quizzing yourself one more time with your list of questions.

PHASE 3: *After you read*

STEP 6: RECITE

When you finish a reading assignment, make a speech about it. Talk to yourself about what you've read. When you recite, you practice synthesis—the process of combining individual ideas and facts into a meaningful whole.

One way to get yourself to recite is to look at the chapter titles and headings in your text. Pick one. Then put the book down and start talking out loud. Explain as much as you can about that particular section of your text.

To make reciting more effective, do it in front of a mirror. It might seem silly, but the benefits can be enormous. Reap them at exam time.

In addition, recite to other people. Classmates are even better than mirrors. Form a study group and practice teaching one another what you have read. One of the best ways to learn anything is to teach it to someone else.

Talk about your reading whenever you can. Tell friends and family members what you're learning.

A related technique is to stop reading periodically and write a short, free-form summary of what you just read. You can recite by writing as well as speaking.

Talking and writing about your reading reinforces a valuable skill—the ability to summarize. This will come in handy for any course you take or career you choose. You'll be able to boil a lot of information down to the key points.

Whatever technique you use, plan to recite within 24 hours of reading new material. Sound the trumpets! This point is critical: Reciting within 24 hours helps move information from your short-term memory to your long-term memory.

So, recite within one day. If you read it on Wednesday, recite it on Thursday. At this time, look over your notes. Clear up anything you don't understand. Recite the main points several times.

This period of reciting can be short. You might spend as little as 15 minutes on a difficult two-hour reading assignment. Investing that time now can save you hours later when studying for exams.

STEP 7: REVIEW

To review, take the process of reciting to a deeper level. Look for quiz questions, sample problems, and lists of key terms at the end of a chapter. Answer those questions, solve those problems, and define those terms in your own words. Then check your answers against the text.

Also consider creating written summaries. Pick one chapter (or one section of one chapter) from any of your textbooks. Write down the main topic covered in this chapter. Then write the main points that the author makes about this topic.

DISCOVERY / INTENTION STATEMENT

Experimenting with Muscle Reading

After experimenting with Muscle Reading, reflect on your reading skills. Are you a more effective reader now? Less effective? Record your observations: I discovered that I . . .

Many students find that they use some but not all of the Muscle Reading steps. Depending on the text, reading assignment, your available time, and your commitment level

to the material, you may discover that including additional steps helps you. Right now, make a commitment to yourself to experiment with specific Muscle Reading steps by completing the following Intention Statement: I intend to use the following Muscle Reading steps for the next two weeks in my _____ class:

☐ Preview   ☐ Flag answers
☐ Outline   ☐ Recite
☐ Question   ☐ Review
☐ Focus   ☐ Review again

For example, the main topic up to this point in this chapter is Muscle Reading. The main point about this topic is that Muscle Reading includes three phases—steps to take before you read, while you read, and after you read. For a more detailed summary, list each of the steps.

Also create flash cards using 3 × 5 cards or an app for your computer or smartphone. Write one question or key term on one side of the card. Write the answer or definition on the other side.

All of these techniques are examples of something that psychologists call *retrieval practice*.[1] Again, the purpose is to take information from short-term memory, consolidate it, and move into your long-term memory. The more times that you retrieve (recall) facts and ideas, the longer you'll remember them.

Note: Retrieval practice looks different when you want to summarize short stories, novels, plays, and other works of fiction. Focus on insight and action. In most stories, the main character confronts a major problem, has an "aha!" moment about how to solve it, and then takes a series of actions. Describe that problem and the character's main insights. Then list the actions that follow—the key plot points in the story.

STEP 8: REVIEW AGAIN

The final step in Muscle Reading is the weekly or monthly review. The purpose of this review is to keep the neural pathways to the information open and to make them more distinct. That way, the information can be easier to recall.

Remember that you can squeeze reviews into small pockets of time. Recite for five minutes while you are waiting for a bus, for your socks to dry, or for the water to boil. These short review periods can be effortless and fun. Keep your flash cards with you so that you can use them anywhere.

Sometimes longer review periods are appropriate. For example, if you found an assignment difficult, consider rereading it. Start over, as if you had never seen the material before. Sometimes a second or third reading will provide you with surprising insights. ✶

Ways to OVERCOME CONFUSION

ESB Professional/Shutterstock.com

Sometimes ordinary reading methods are not enough. It's easy to get bogged down in a murky reading assignment. The solution starts with a First Step: When you are confused, tell the truth about it.

Successful readers monitor their understanding of reading material. They do not see confusion as a mistake or a personal shortcoming. Instead, they take it as a cue to change reading strategies and process ideas at a deeper level.

Read it again. Somehow, students get the idea that reading means opening a book and dutifully slogging through the text—line by line, page by page. They move in a straight line from the first word until the last. Actually, this method can be an ineffective way to read much of the material you'll encounter in college.

Feel free to shake up your routine. Make several passes through tough reading material. During a preview, for example, just scan the text to look for key words and highlighted material. Next, skim the entire chapter or article again, spending a little more time and taking in more than you did during your preview. Finally, read in more depth, proceeding word by word through some or all of the text. Difficult material—such as the technical writing in science texts—is often easier the second time around. Isolate difficult passages and read them again, slowly.

This suggestion comes with one caution. If you find yourself doing a lot of rereading, then consider a change in reading strategies. For example, you might benefit from reciting after each section rather than after each chapter.

Look for essential words. If you are stuck on a paragraph, mentally cross out the adjectives and adverbs and read the sentences without them. Find the important words—usually verbs and nouns.

Hold a mini-review. Pause briefly to summarize—either verbally or in writing—what you've read so far. Stop at the end of a paragraph, and recite, in your own words, what you have just read. Jot down some notes, or create a short outline or summary.

Read it out loud. Make noise. Read a passage out loud several times, each time using a different inflection and emphasizing a different part of the sentence. Be creative. Imagine that you are the author talking.

Talk to someone who can help. Admit when you are stuck. Then bring questions about reading assignments to classmates and members of your study group. Also, make an appointment with your instructor. Ask for the "big picture" of your reading assignment—the main questions it raises and answers. Then

Five ways to read with children underfoot

It is possible to have both effective study time and quality time with your children. The following suggestions come mostly from students who are also parents. The specific strategies you use will depend on your schedule and the ages of your children.

Find a regular playmate for your child. Some children can pair off with close friends and safely retreat to their rooms for hours of private play. You can check on them occasionally and still get lots of reading done.

Create a special space for your child. Set aside one room or area of your home as a play space. Childproof this space. The goal is to create a place where children can roam freely and play with minimal supervision. Consider allowing your child in this area *only* when you study. Your homework time then becomes your child's reward. If you're cramped for space, just set aside some special toys for your child to play with during your study time.

Use television responsibly. Whenever possible, select educational programs that keep your child's mind active and engaged. Also see whether your child can use headphones while watching television. That way, the house stays quiet while you study.

Schedule time to be with your children when you've finished studying. Let your children in on the plan: "I'll be done reading at seven thirty. That gives us a whole hour to play before you go to bed."

Ask other adults for help. Getting help can be as simple as asking your spouse, partner, neighbor, or fellow student to take care of your children while you study. Offer to trade childcare with a neighbor: You will take his kids and yours for two hours on Thursday night if he'll take them for two hours on Saturday morning.

Find community activities and services. Ask whether your school provides a childcare service. In some cases, these services are available to students at a reduced cost.

move on to specific points of confusion. Point out the sentences and paragraphs that you don't understand.

Stand up. Changing positions periodically can combat fatigue. Experiment with standing as you read, especially if you get stuck on a tough passage and decide to read it out loud.

Skip around. Jump to the next section or to the end of a tough article or

chapter. You might have lost the big picture. Simply seeing the next step, the next main point, or a summary might be all you need to put the details in context. Retrace the steps in a chain of ideas, and look for examples. Absorb facts and ideas in whatever order works for you—which may be different from the author's presentation.

Find a tutor. Many schools provide free tutoring services. If your school does not, other students who have completed the course can assist you.

Use another text. Find a similar text in the library. Sometimes a concept is easier to understand if it is expressed another way. Children's books—especially children's encyclopedias—can provide useful overviews of baffling subjects. Also do an Internet search using the title of the article or book. Look for summaries and comments on the text from sources that you trust.

Note where you get stuck. When you feel stuck, stop reading for a moment and diagnose what's happening. At these stop points, mark your place in the margin of the page with an "S" for *Stuck*. A pattern to your marks over several pages might indicate a question you want to answer before going further.

Construct a word stack. Sometimes the source of confusion is an unfamiliar word. When you come across one, write it down on a 3 × 5 card. Below the word, copy the sentence in which it was used and the page number. You can look up each word immediately, or you can accumulate a stack of these cards and look up the words later. Write the definition of each word on the back of the 3 × 5 card, adding the diacritics—marks that tell you how to pronounce the word.

Divide unfamiliar words into parts. Another strategy for expanding your vocabulary is to divide an unfamiliar word into syllables and look for familiar parts. This strategy works well if you make it a point to learn common prefixes (beginning syllables) and suffixes (ending syllables). For example, the suffix *-tude* usually refers to a condition or state of being. Knowing this makes it easier to conclude that *habitude* refers to a repeated way of doing something. Likewise, *similitude* means being similar or having a quality of resemblance.

Infer the meaning of words from their context. You can often deduce the meaning of an unfamiliar word simply by paying attention to its context—the surrounding words, phrases, sentences, paragraphs, or images. Later, you can confirm your deduction by consulting a dictionary.

Practice looking for context clues such as these:

- **Definitions.** A key word might be defined in the text. Look for phrases such as *defined as* or *in other words*.

- **Examples.** Authors often provide examples to clarify a word meaning. If the word is not explicitly defined, then study the examples. They're often preceded by the phrases *for example, for instance,* or *such as.*

- **Lists.** When a word is listed in a series, pay attention to the other items in the series. They might define the unfamiliar word through association.

- **Comparisons.** You might find a new word surrounded by synonyms—words with a similar meaning. Look for synonyms after words such as *like* and *as.*

- **Contrasts.** A writer might juxtapose a word with its antonym. Look for phrases such as *on the contrary* and *on the other hand.*

Stop reading. When none of the suggestions work, do not despair. Admit your confusion, and then take a break. Catch a movie, go for a walk, study another subject, or sleep on it. The concepts you've already absorbed might come together at a subconscious level as you move on to other activities. Allow some time for that process. When you return to the reading material, see it with fresh eyes. ✂

SKILLS
snapshot

After studying this chapter, you might want to make some changes to the way you read. First, take a snapshot of your current reading habits, and reflect on the reading skills you've already developed. Complete the following sentences.

Discovery

My score on the Reading section of the Discovery Wheel was . . .

When it's important for me to remember what I read, I . . .

When I don't understand something that I've read, I overcome confusion by . . .

Intention

I'll know that I've reached a new level of mastery with reading when . . .

Stated as a goal, my intention is to . . .

Action

To reach my goal, the most important habits that I can practice are . . .

do you have a
MINUTE

Make it a habit to include 60-second tasks in your action statements. For reading, here are some examples:

- Skim the headings in one textbook chapter.
- Turn one heading in one of your textbooks into a question.
- Based on your reading, recite an answer to that question.
- In the margin of a textbook chapter or article, number the steps in a process.
- Skim one article that you've bookmarked online.

*Show up for class
both physically and
mentally. Your job
is to observe an
event, which can
be anything from
a lecture to a lab
experiment or a
slide show of an
artist's works.*

Dragon Images/Shutterstock.com

Participating in Class & Taking Notes

why

Note taking helps you remember information and influences how well you do on tests.

how

Recall a recent incident in which you had difficulty taking notes. Perhaps you were listening to an instructor who talked fast, or you got confused and stopped taking notes altogether. Then preview this chapter to find at least three strategies that you can use right away to take better notes.

what if...

I could take notes that remain informative and useful for weeks, months, or even years to come?

what is included ...

do you have a minute?

Look at today's notes from a course that you're taking this term. Take a minute to do a quick edit. For instance, fix passages that are illegible. Label the notes with the date and the name of the class. If you a few seconds to spare, then number the pages.

I create it all

This article describes a powerful tool for times of trouble. In a crisis, "I create it all" can lead the way to solutions. The main point of this Power Process is to treat experiences, events, and circumstances in your life *as if* you created them.

"I create it all" is one of the most unusual and bizarre suggestions in this text. It certainly is not a belief. Use it when it works. Don't when it doesn't. Keeping that in mind, consider how powerful this Power Process can be. It is really about the difference between two distinct positions in life: being a victim or being responsible.

A victim of circumstances is controlled by outside forces. We've all felt like victims at one time or another. Sometimes we felt helpless.

In contrast, we can take responsibility. Responsibility is "response-ability"—the ability to choose a *response* to any event. You can choose your *response* to any event, even when the event itself is beyond your control.

Many students approach grades from the position of being victims. When the student who sees the world this way gets an F, she reacts probably like this:

"Another F! That teacher couldn't teach her way out of a wet paper bag. She can't teach English for anything. There's no way to take notes in that class. And that textbook—what a bore!"

The problem with this viewpoint is that in looking for excuses, the student is robbing herself of the power to get any grade other than an F. She's giving all of her power to a bad teacher and a boring textbook.

There is another way, called *taking responsibility*. You can recognize that you choose your grades by choosing your actions. Then you are the source, rather than the result, of the grades you get. The student who got an F could react like this:

"Another F! Oh, shoot! Well, hmmm . . . What did I do to create it?"

Now, that's power. By asking, "How did I contribute to this outcome?" you are no longer the victim. This student might continue by saying, "Well, let's see. I didn't review my notes after class. That might have done it." Or, "I went out with my friends the night before the test. Well, that probably helped me fulfill some of the requirements for getting an F."

The point is this: When the F is the result of your friends, the book, or the teacher, you probably can't do anything about it. However, if you *chose* the F, you can choose a different grade next time. You are in charge. ▰

NOTE-TAKING
essentials

You enter a lecture hall filled with students. For the next hour, one person standing at the front of the room will do most of the talking. Everyone else is seated and silent, taking notes. The lecturer seems to be doing all the work.

Don't be deceived. Look closely and you'll see students taking notes in a way that radiates energy. They're awake and alert. They're writing—a physical activity that expresses mental engagement.

One way to understand note taking is to realize that taking notes is just one part of the process. Effective note taking consists of three phases:

- **First, you carefully set the stage for taking notes.** This means showing up for class both physically and mentally. Your job is to observe an event, which can be anything from a lecture to a lab experiment or a slide show of an artist's works.
- **Second, you record your observations of that event.** That is, you "take notes." This means listening for the main points and capturing them in the form of key words and images. Master students like to play with various formats for note taking, often discovering that a change in approach can deepen their understanding of course material.
- **Third, you return to your notes at a later time to mine them for added value.** You review what you have recorded. You memorize, reflect, and apply what you're learning. In addition, you predict test questions and rehearse possible answers. All this activity lifts ideas off the page and turns them into a working part of your mind.

Each phase of the note-taking process is essential, and each depends on the others. Setting the stage determines the quality of your observations. And the quality of the words and images that you capture determines how much value you can extract from your notes.

Legible and speedy handwriting, knowledge about outlining, a nifty pen, and a new notebook are all great note-taking devices. Technology—including laptop computers, tablets, and smartphones—takes traditional note taking to a whole new level. You can capture key notes with word-processing, outlining, database, or publishing software—and an ever-expanding catalog of mobile apps. Your notes can become living documents that you access at any time from a variety of devices. You can search, bookmark, tag, and archive the content of your notes as you would do with other digital files.

Nikodash/Shutterstock.com

And all those tools are worthwhile only if you take notes in a way that helps you *understand* what you read and what you experience in class.

This is a well-researched aspect of student success in higher education. Study after study points to the benefits of taking notes. The value is added in two ways. First, you create a set of materials that refreshes your memory and helps you prepare for tests. Second, taking notes prompts you to listen effectively during class. You translate new ideas into your own words and images. You impose a personal and meaningful structure on what you see, read, and hear. You move from passive observer to active participant.[1] It's not that you take notes so that you can learn from them later. Instead, you learn *while* taking notes.

Remember that good note taking calls for effort. It requires you to think rather than just passively record information. The goal is not to capture everything that you hear or read. Instead, distinguish between the main points and supporting details. Focus on big ideas—not isolated facts. You'll take fewer notes, and they'll be better notes.

While in school, you may spend hundreds of hours taking notes. Experimenting with ways to make those notes more effective is a direct investment in your success. Think of your notes as a textbook that you create—one that's more in tune with your learning preferences than any textbook you could buy.

Use the suggestions in this chapter to complete each phase of note taking more effectively. If you put these ideas into practice, you can turn even the most disorganized chicken scratches into tools for learning. ✄

SET THE STAGE

for note taking

A. and I. Kruk/Shutterstock.com

The process of note taking begins well before you enter a classroom or crack open a book. Promote your success by "psyching up"—setting the physical and mental stage to receive what your teachers have to offer.

Also remember that your ability to take notes in any course improves when you attend class regularly, keep up with assignments, and truly show up to learn. That means taking a seat in the room *and* focusing your attention while you're there. Use the following suggestions to meet these goals.

COMPLETE REQUIRED READING

Instructors usually assume that students complete reading assignments, and they construct their lectures accordingly. The more familiar you are with a subject, the easier it will be to understand in class.

PACK MATERIALS

A good pen does not make you a good observer, but the lack of a pen, a notebook, or other note-taking tools can disrupt your concentration. Make sure you have any materials you will need, including a textbook.

ARRIVE EARLY TO PUT YOUR BRAIN IN GEAR

Arriving to class late or with only seconds to spare can add a level of stress that interferes with listening. Avoid that interference by arriving at least five minutes before class begins. Use this spare time to review notes from the previous class session.

SIT IN THE FRONT OF THE CLASSROOM

The closer you sit to the front, the fewer the distractions. Also, material on the board is easier to read from up front, and the instructor can see you more easily when you have a question.

TAKE CARE OF HOUSEKEEPING DETAILS

If you're taking notes on paper, then write your name and phone number in each notebook in case you lose it. Class notes become more valuable as a term proceeds. Develop the habit of labeling and dating your notes at the beginning of each class. Number the pages too.

Devote a specific section of your notebook to listing assignments for each course. Keep all details about test dates here also, along with a course syllabus. You're less likely to forget assignments if you compile them in one place where you can review them all at a glance.

Leave blank space. Notes tightly crammed on the page are hard to read and difficult to review. Leave plenty of space on the page. Later, when you review, you can use the blank space to clarify points, write questions, or add other material.

Use a three-ring binder for paper-based notes. Three-ring binders give you several benefits. First, pages can be removed and spread out when you review. Second, the three-ring-binder format will allow you to insert handouts right into your notes easily. Third, you can insert your own out-of-class notes in the correct order.

Use only one side of a piece of paper. When you use one side of a page, you can review and organize all your notes by spreading them out side by side.

LIMIT DISTRACTIONS

Listening well can be defined as the process of overcoming distraction. In the classroom, you may have to deal with external distractions—noises from the next room, other students' conversations, or a lecturer who speaks softly. Internal distractions can be even more potent—for example, stress, memories about last night's party, or daydreams about what you'll do after class.

When the distraction is external, the solution may be obvious. Move closer to the front of the room, ask the lecturer to speak up, or politely ask classmates to keep quiet. Internal distractions can be trickier. Some solutions follow.

Flood your mind with sensory data. Notice the shape of your pen. Feel the surface of your desk. Bring yourself back to class by paying attention to the temperature or the quality of light in the room.

Notice and release daydreams. If your attention wanders, don't grit your teeth and try to stay focused. Just notice when your attention has wandered and gently bring it back.

Pause for a few seconds, and write distracting thoughts down. If you're thinking about the errands you want to run later, list them on a 3 × 5 card. Once your distractions are out of your mind and safely stored on paper, you can gently return your attention to taking notes.

Let go of judgments about lecture styles. Human beings are judgment machines. We evaluate everything, especially other people. We notice the way someone looks or speaks, and we instantly make up a story about her. We do this so quickly that we don't even realize it.

Don't let your attitude about an instructor's lecture style, habits, or appearance get in the way of your education. You can decrease the power of your judgments if you pay attention to them and let them go.

You can even let go of judgments about rambling, unorganized lectures. Take the initiative, and organize the material yourself. While taking notes, separate the key points from the examples and supporting evidence. Note the places where you got confused, and make a list of questions to ask.

Participate in class activities. Ask questions. Volunteer for demonstrations. Join in class discussions. Be willing to take a risk or look foolish if that's what it takes for you to learn. Chances are, the question you think is "dumb" is also on the minds of several of your classmates.

Relate the class to your goals. If you have trouble staying awake in a particular class, write at the top of your notes how that class relates to a specific goal. Identify the payoff for reaching that goal.

REMEMBER THAT YOU CAN LISTEN *AND* DISAGREE

When you hear something you disagree with, notice your disagreement and let it go. If your disagreement is persistent and strong, make note of this, and then move on. Internal debate can prevent you from receiving new information. Just absorb it with a mental tag: "I don't agree, but my instructor says . . ."

When you review your notes later, think critically about the instructor's ideas. List questions or note your disagreements.

Also avoid "listening with your answer running." This refers to the habit of forming your response to people's ideas *before* they've finished speaking. Let the speaker have his or her say, even when you're sure you'll disagree.

COPE WITH FAST-TALKING TEACHERS

Ask the instructor to slow down. This obvious suggestion is easily forgotten. If asking him to slow down doesn't work, ask him to repeat what you missed. Also experiment with the following suggestions.

Take more time to prepare for class. Familiarity with a subject increases your ability to pick out key points. Before class, take detailed notes on your reading, and leave plenty of blank space. Take these notes with you to class, and simply add your lecture notes to them.

Be willing to make choices. Focus your attention on key points. Instead of trying to write everything down, choose what you think is important. Occasionally, you will make a wrong choice and neglect an important point. Worse things could happen.

Exchange copies of notes with classmates. Your fellow students might write down something you missed. At the same time, your notes might help them.

Leave empty spaces in your notes. Allow plenty of room for filling in information you missed. Use a symbol that signals you've missed something, so you can remember to come back to it.

See the instructor after class. Take your class notes with you, and show the instructor what you missed.

Learn shorthand. Some note-taking systems, known as shorthand, are specifically designed for getting ideas down fast. Books and courses are available to help you learn these systems.

Ask questions even if you're totally lost. There may be times when you feel so lost that you can't even formulate a question. That's okay. Just report this fact to the instructor. Or just ask any question. Often this will lead you to the question that you really want to ask.

GIVE THE SPEAKER FEEDBACK

Speakers thrive on attention. Give lecturers verbal and nonverbal feedback—everything from simple eye contact to insightful comments and questions. Such feedback can raise an instructor's energy level and improve the class.

BRACKET EXTRA MATERIAL

Bracketing refers to separating your own thoughts from the lecturer's as you take notes. This is useful in two circumstances.

First, bracket your own opinions. For the most part, avoid making editorial comments in your lecture notes. The danger is that when you return to your notes, you may mistake your own ideas for those of the speaker. Clearly label your own comments, such as questions to ask later or strong disagreements. Pick a symbol, like brackets, and use it consistently.

Second, bracket material that confuses you. Invent your own signal for getting lost during a lecture. For example, write a circled question mark in the margin of the paper. Or simply leave space for the explanation that you will get later. This space will also be a signal that you missed something. Be honest with yourself when you don't understand. ✖

Take a pause right now to gather your essential note-taking materials. Place them in a backpack, briefcase, or bag that you always take with you.

Capture
KEY WORDS

When it comes to notes, more is not necessarily better.

Your job is not to write down all of a lecturer's words or even most of them. Taking effective notes calls for split-second decisions about which words are essential to record and which are less important.

An easy way to sort the less important from the essential is to take notes using key words. Key words or phrases contain the essence of communication. They include technical terms, names, numbers, equations, and words of degree: *most, least, faster,* and the like.

Key words are laden with associations. They evoke images and associations with other words and ideas. One key word can initiate the recall of a whole cluster of ideas. A few key words can form a chain: From those words, you can reconstruct an entire lecture.

FOCUS ON NOUNS AND VERBS

In many languages, there are two types of words that carry the essential meaning of most sentences—nouns and verbs. For example, the previous sentence could be reduced to *nouns verbs carry meaning. Carry* is a verb; most of the remaining words are nouns.

There are additional ways to subtract words from your notes and still retain the lecturer's meaning:

Eliminate adverbs and adjectives.
The words *extremely interesting* can become *interesting* in your notes—or simply an exclamation mark (!).

VikiVector/Shutterstock.com

Note the topic followed by a colon and key point. For instance, *There are seven key principles that can help you take effective notes* becomes *Effective notes: 7 principles.*

Use lists. There are two basic types. A numbered list expresses steps that need to be completed in a certain order. A simple bulleted list includes ideas that are related but do not have to follow a sequential order.

Look for models. To find more examples of key words, study newspaper headlines. Good headlines include a verb and only enough nouns to communicate the essence of an event or idea.

To see how key words can be used in note taking, take yourself to an imaginary classroom. You are enrolled in a course on world religion, and today's lecture is an introduction to Buddhism. The instructor begins with these words:

Okay, today we're going to talk about three core precepts of Buddhism. I know that this is a religion that may not be familiar to many of you, and I ask that you keep an open mind as I proceed. Now, with that caveat out of the way, let's move ahead.

First, let's look at the term anicca. By the way, this word is spelled a-n-i-c-c-a. Everybody got that? Great. All right, well, this is a word in an ancient language called Pali, which was widely spoken in India during the Buddha's time—about 600 years before the birth of Jesus. Anicca is a word layered with many meanings and is almost impossible to translate into English. If you read books about Buddhism, you may see it rendered as impermanence, *and this is a passable translation.*

Impermanence is something that you can observe directly in your everyday experience. Look at any object in your external environment, and you'll find that it's constantly changing. Even the most solid and stable things—like a mountain, for example—are dynamic. You could use time-lapse photography to record images of a mountain every day for 10 years, and if you did, you'd see incredible change— rocks shifting, mudslides, new vegetation, and the like.

Following is one way to reduce this section of the lecture to key words:

> *Buddhism: 3 concepts*
> *#1 = anicca = impermanence.*
> *Anicca = Pali = ancient Indian language (600 yrs b4 Jesus).*
> *Example of anicca: time-lapse photos @ changes in mountain.*

In this case the original 200+ words of the lecture are now less than 30. However, this example might be a little sparse for your tastes. Remember that it shows only one possible option for abbreviating your notes. Don't take it as a model to imitate strictly.

A CAVEAT: USE COMPLETE SENTENCES AT CRUCIAL POINTS

Sometimes key words aren't enough. When an instructor repeats a sentence slowly and emphasizes each word, she's sending you a signal. Also, technical definitions are often worded precisely because even a slightly different wording renders the definitions useless or incorrect. Write down key sentences word for word.

IN ADDITION …

Write notes in paragraphs with complete sentences. When it is difficult to follow the organization of a lecture or to put information into outline form, create a series of informal paragraphs. Use complete sentences for precise definitions, direct quotations, and important points that the instructor emphasizes by repetition or other signals—such as the phrase "This is an important point." For other material, focus on capturing key words.

Listen for introductory, concluding, and transition words and phrases. Examples are "the following three factors," "in conclusion," "the most important consideration," "in addition to," and "on the other hand." These phrases and similar ones signal relationships, definitions, new subjects, conclusions, cause-and-effect, and examples. They reveal the structure of the lecture. You can use these phrases to organize your notes.

Take notes in different colors. You can use colors as highly visible organizers. For example, you can signal important points with red. Or use one color for notes about the text and another color for lecture notes. Besides, notes that are visually pleasing can be easier to review.

Copy key material. Choose when to record information exactly as an instructor presents it. Record formulas, diagrams, problems, and quotations that the teacher presents on the board or in a PowerPoint presentation. Copy dates, numbers, names, places, and other key facts. If it's presented visually in class, put it in your notes. You can even use your own signal or code to flag that material.

Plan to get notes for classes you miss. For most courses, you'll benefit by attending every class session. If you miss a class, catch up as quickly as possible. Early in each term, connect with other students who are willing to share notes. Also contact your instructor. Perhaps there is another section of the same course that you can attend so you won't miss the lecture information. If there is a website for your class, check it for assignments and the availability of handouts you missed. ✳

do you have a
MINUTE?

Take a break right now to create a list of abbreviations that you will use for note taking.

PLAY

with note-taking formats

Choose a format for taking notes that prompts you to *organize* information as you record it. Doing this will enhance your memory and save time when you review your notes later.

This article presents three popular methods—the Cornell format, outlines, and concept maps. Experiment with each to discover what works for you.

THE CORNELL FORMAT

This method is named after Walter Pauk, who taught at Cornell University.[2] The cornerstone of this system is simple: a wide margin on the left-hand side of the page. Pauk calls this the *cue column*, and using it is the key to the Cornell format's many benefits. To get started with this approach to note taking, review Figure 4.1, and then take the following steps.

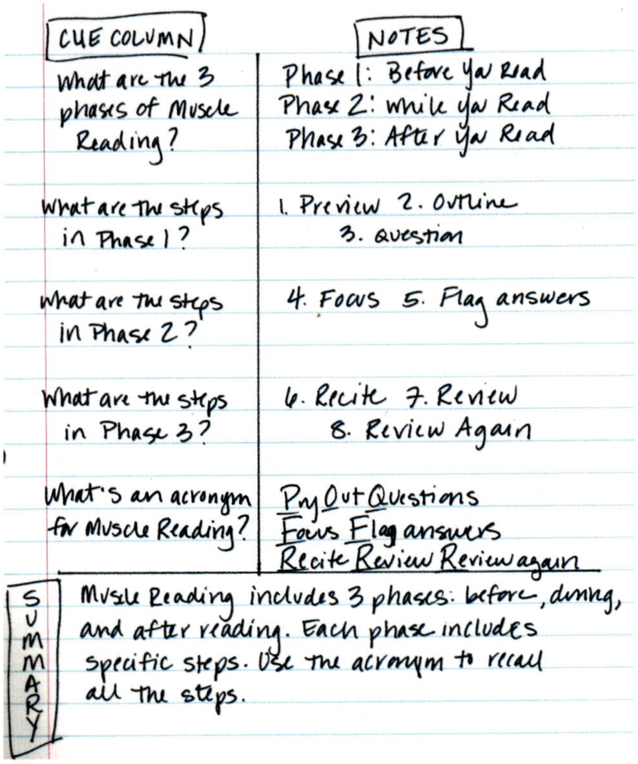

Format your paper. On each page of your notes, draw a vertical line, top to bottom, about two inches from the left edge of the paper. This line creates the cue column—the space to the left of the line. You will use this space later to condense and review your notes.

Pauk also suggests that you leave a two-inch space at the bottom of the page. He calls this the summary area. This space is also designed to be used at a later stage, as you review your notes.

Take notes, leaving the cue column and summary area blank. As you read or listen to a lecture, take notes on the right-hand side of the page. *Do not write in the cue column or summary area.* You'll use these spaces later.

Fill in the cue column. You can reduce your notes to several kinds of entries in the cue column:

- *Key questions.* Think of the notes you took on the right-hand side of the page as a set of answers. In the cue column, write the corresponding questions. Write one question for each major term or point in your notes.
- *Key words.* Writing key words will speed the review process later. Also, reading your notes and focusing on extracting key words will further reinforce your understanding of the lecture or reading assignment.
- *Headings.* Pretend that you are a copy editor at a newspaper and that the notes you took are a series of articles about different topics. In the cue column, write a headline

Figure 4.1 **Cornell Notes**

for each "article." Use actual newspaper headlines—and headings in your textbooks—as models.

Fill in the summary area. See whether you can reduce all the notes on the page to a sentence or two. Add cross-references to topics elsewhere in your notes that are closely related. Explain briefly why the notes on this page matter; if you think the material is likely to appear on a test, note that fact here. Also, use the summary area to list any questions that you want to ask in class.

OUTLINES

In addition to the Cornell format, another option for note taking is outlining. Use this tool to organize your notes from general to specific. The classic method is to use specific characters and indentation to signal each level of information:

- Place *roman numerals* in front of the major topics that are presented in a lecture or reading assignment.
- Place *capital letters* in front of the main points about those topics.
- Place *numbers* in front of facts, examples, and other details that support the main points.

Figure 4.2 is a sample outline for the steps of Muscle Reading:

You can also create effective outlines without Roman numerals. For example, record topics in all-capital letters. Place a dash in front of main points. And place a bullet point in front of each supporting detail.

CONCEPT MAPS

Concept mapping—explained by Joseph Novak and D. Bob Gowin in their book *Learning How to Learn*—is a way to express ideas in a visual form.[3] Here are the key elements:

- A main concept written at the top of a page
- Related concepts arranged in a hierarchy, with more general concepts toward the top of a page and more specific concepts toward the bottom

Figure 4.2 Outline with Roman Numerals

First-level heading
I. Phase One: Before You Read
Second-level heading
  A. Preview
Third-level heading
   1. Words in boldface or italics
   2. Visuals
  B. Outline
  C. Question
II. While You Read
  A. Focus
  B. Flag Answers
   1. Underline
   2. Highlight
III. After You Read
  A. Recite
  B. Review
  C. Review Again

- Links—lines with words that briefly explain the relationship between concepts

When you combine concepts with their linking words, you'll often get complete sentences (or sets of coherent phrases). One benefit of concept maps is that they quickly,

Short and sweet—remember to abrevi8

Abbreviations can be useful in note taking as well as texting—if you use them consistently. Some abbreviations are standard. If you make up your own abbreviations, write a key explaining them in your notes.

Avoid vague abbreviations. When you use an abbreviation like *comm.* for *committee,* you run the risk of not being able to remember whether you meant *committee, commission, common, commit, community, communicate,* or *communist.*

The following seven principles explain how to use abbreviations in your notes:

Principle: Leave out articles.
Examples: Omit *a, an, the.*

Principle: Leave out vowels.
Examples: *Talk* becomes *tlk; said* becomes *sd.*

Principle: Use mathematical symbols.
Examples: *Plus* becomes +; minus becomes −; *is more than* becomes >; *is less than* becomes <; *equals, are, or is* becomes =.

Principle: Use arrows to indicate causation or a combination of factors that creates a change.
Examples: *Causes, leads to, or shows that* becomes →

Principle: Use standard abbreviations, and omit the periods.
Examples: *Pound* becomes *lb; Avenue* becomes *ave.*

Principle: Create words from numbers and letters that you can sound out and combine.
Examples: *Before* becomes *b4; too* becomes *2.*

Principle: Use a comma in place of *and.*
Example: *Freud and Jung were major figures in twentieth-century psychology* becomes *20th century psych: Freud, Jung = major figures.*

Note: If you key your notes into computer files, you can often use a Find and Replace command to replace abbreviations with full words.

vividly, and accurately show the relationships between ideas. Figure 4.3 is a sample concept map based on a reading assignment about nutrition.

COMBINE FORMATS

Feel free to use different note-taking systems for different subjects and to combine formats. Do what works for you.

For example, combine concept maps along with the Cornell method. You can modify the Cornell format by dividing your notepaper in half. Reserve half for concept maps and the other half for linear information such as lists, graphs, and outlines, as well as equations, long explanations, and word-for-word definitions.

You can also include a concept map into your paragraph-style notes whenever you feel one is appropriate. Concept maps are also useful for summarizing notes taken in the Cornell format.

Another option is to write free-form notes in paragraphs, lists, or maps. Spend 10 minutes writing down everything you remember from one of today's classes. Then compare these notes to the notes that you actually took in class. Look for differences and reconcile them.

Also make time to *condense* your notes. Once per week, take your class notes for each course and summarize them on *one* sheet of paper. The limited space forces you to list

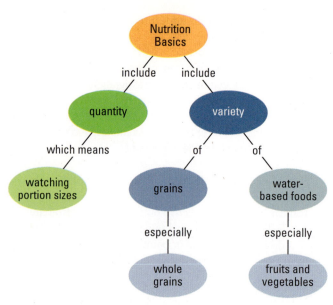

Figure 4.3 **Concept Map**

only the main concepts and key supporting details. Draw lines and arrows to indicate how concepts are related. This is a powerful way to prepare for tests and an excellent activity for study groups. ✺

WAYS TO PREDICT

test questions

Predicting test questions can do more than help you get better grades. It can also keep you focused on the purpose of the course and help you design your learning strategies.

Following are legal and constructive ways to outsmart your teacher and reduce surprises at test time.

GO AHEAD AND ASK

Eliminate as much guesswork as possible. Ask your instructor to describe upcoming tests. Here are some questions to ask:

- What course material will the test cover—readings, lectures, lab sessions, or a combination?
- Will the test be cumulative, or will it cover just the most recent material you've studied?
- Will the test focus on facts and details or major themes and relationships?
- Will the test call on you to solve problems or apply concepts?
- Will you have choices about which questions to answer?
- What types of questions will be on the test—true/false, multiple choice, short answer, essay?

Note: To study appropriately for essay tests, find out how much detail the instructor wants in your answers. Ask how much time you'll be allowed for the test and about the length of essay answers (number of pages, blue books, or word limit). Having that information before you begin studying will help you gauge your depth for learning the material.

NOTICE VERBAL CUES FROM YOUR TEACHER

Few teachers will try to disguise the main content of their courses. In fact, most offer repeated clues about what they want you to remember. Many of those clues are verbal.

Repetition. Your teachers may state important points several times or return to those points in subsequent classes. They may also read certain passages word for word from their notes or from a book. Be sure to record all these points fully in your notes.

Common terms. Also note your teachers' "pet phrases"—repeated terms that relate directly to course content. You could benefit from using these terms in essay exams—along with explanations in your own words to show that you truly understand the concepts.

Questions. Pay attention to questions that the instructor poses to the class. These are potential test questions.

Write them down, along with some answers.

Emphasis on certain types of content. Some teachers emphasize details—facts, names, dates, technical terms, and the like. Other teachers focus on broad themes and major events. Be alert to such differences. They are clues to the kind of tests you'll have.

Placement of content. Listen closely to material presented at the beginning and end of a lecture. Skilled speakers often preview or review their key content at these points.

Comments on assigned readings. When material from reading assignments is also covered extensively in class, it is likely to be on the test. The opposite can also be true: When your teacher emphasizes material that does *not* appear in any assigned reading, that material is likely to be important.

NOTICE NONVERBAL CUES FROM YOUR TEACHER

Sometimes a lecturer's body language will give potent clues to key content. He might use certain gestures when making critical points—pausing, looking down at notes, staring at the ceiling,

or searching for words. If the lecturer has to think hard about how to make a point, that's probably an important point. Also note the following:

Watch the board or screen. If an instructor takes time to write something down and display it to the whole class, consider this to be another signal that the material is important. In short: If it's on the board, on a screen, or in a handout, put it in your notes. Use your own signal or code to flag this material.

Watch the instructor's eyes. If an instructor glances at his notes and then makes a point, it is probably a signal that the information is especially important. Anything he reads from his notes is a potential test question.

Remember the obvious. Listen for these words: "This material will be on the test."

REVIEW YOUR PREDICTIONS

Create a signal to flag possible test items in your notes. Use asterisks (**), exclamation marks (!!), or a *T!* in a circle. Place these signals in the margin next to ideas that seem like possible test items. Give these items special attention while you review your notes. ✴

Turn PowerPoints into
POWERFUL NOTES

PowerPoint presentations are common. They can also be lethal for students who want to master course content—or those who simply want to stay awake.

Some students stop taking notes during a PowerPoint presentation. This choice can be hazardous to your academic health for three major reasons:

- *PowerPoint presentations don't include everything.* Instructors and other speakers use PowerPoint to organize their presentations. Topics covered in the slides make up an outline of what your instructor considers important. Slides are created to flag the main points and signal transitions between points. However, speakers usually add examples and explanations that don't appear on the slides. In addition, slides will not include any material from class discussion, including any answers that the instructor gives in response to questions.

- *You stop learning.* Taking notes forces you to capture ideas and information in your own words. Also, the act of writing things down helps you remember the material. If you stop writing and let your attention drift, you can quickly get lost.
- *You end up with major gaps in your notes.* When it's time to review your notes, you'll find that material from PowerPoint presentations is missing. This can be a major pain at exam time.

To create value from PowerPoint presentations, take notes on them. Continue to observe, record, and review. See PowerPoint as a way to *guide* rather than to *replace* your own note taking. Even the slickest, smartest presentation is no substitute for your own thinking.

Experiment with the following suggestions. They include ideas about what to do before, during, and after a Power-Point presentation.

BEFORE THE PRESENTATION

Sometimes instructors make PowerPoint slides available before a lecture. If you have computer access, download these files. Scan the slides, just as you would preview a reading assignment.

Consider printing out the slides and bringing them along to class. (If you own a copy of PowerPoint, then choose the Handouts option when printing. This will save paper and ink.) You can take notes directly on the pages that you print out, as in Figure 4.4. Be sure to add the slide numbers if they are missing.

If you use a laptop computer for taking notes during class, then you might not want to bother with printing. Just open up the PowerPoint file, and type your notes in the window that appears at the bottom of each slide. After class, you can print out the slides in note view. This will show the original slides plus any text that you added.

DURING THE PRESENTATION

In many cases, PowerPoint slides are presented visually by the instructor *only during class*. The slides are not provided as handouts, and they are not available online for students to print out.

This makes it even more important to take effective notes in class. Capture the main points and key details as you normally would. Use your preferred note-taking strategies.

Be selective in what you write down. Determine what kind of material is on each slide. Stay alert for new topics, main points, and important details. Taking too many notes makes it hard to keep up with a speaker and separate main points from minor details.

In any case, go *beyond* the slides. Record valuable questions and answers that come up during a discussion, even if they are not a planned part of the presentation.

AFTER THE PRESENTATION

If you printed out slides before class and took notes on those pages, then find a way to integrate them with the rest of your notes. For example, copy key passages from the slides directly into your notes. Add references to specific slides. Or create summary notes that include the major topics and points from readings, class meetings, and PowerPoint presentations.

Printouts of slides can provide review tools. Use them as cues to recite. Cover up your notes so that only the main image or words on each slide are visible. See whether you can remember what else appears on the slide, along with the key points from any notes you added.

Also consider "editing" the presentation. If you have the PowerPoint file on your computer, make another copy of it. Open up this copy, and see whether you can condense the presentation. Cut slides that don't include anything you want to remember. If several slides that develop one point are in a row, then condense all this information on a single slide. Also rearrange slides so that the order makes more sense to you. Remember that you can open up the original file later if you want to see exactly what your instructor presented. ✳

How Muscle Reading Works

▸ Phase 1 – Before You Read
  ▪ **Pry Out Questions**

▸ Phase 2 – While You Read
  ▪ **Focus and Flag Answers**

▸ Phase 3 – After You Read
  ▪ **Recite, Review, and Review Again**

Figure 4.4 Sample PowerPoint slide

Transform your note taking

Think back on the last few lectures you have attended. How would you rate your note-taking skills? As you complete this exercise, think of areas that need improvement.

Discovery Statement
First, recall a recent incident in which you had difficulty taking notes. Perhaps you were listening to an instructor who talked fast. Maybe you got confused and stopped taking notes altogether. Or perhaps you went to review your notes after class, only to find that they made no sense at all.

Describe this incident in more detail, noting how it was challenging for you.

I discovered that . . .

Intention Statement
Now review this chapter to find at least five strategies that you can use right away to help you take better notes. Sum up each of those strategies in a few words, and note the page numbers where these strategies are explained.

Strategy	Page number

Action Statement
Now gear up for action. Describe a specific situation in which you will apply at least one of the strategies you listed previously. If possible, choose a situation that will occur within the next 24 hours.

After experimenting with these strategies, evaluate how well they worked for you. If you thought of a way to modify any of the strategies so that they can work more effectively, describe those modifications.

Take a snapshot of your note-taking skills as they exist today, after reading and doing this chapter. Begin by reflecting on some of your recent experiences with note taking. Then take the next step toward mastery by committing to a specific action in the near future.

Discovery

My score on the Notes section of the Discovery Wheel was . . .

In general, I find my notes to be most useful when they . . .

Intention

I'll know that I've reached a new level of mastery with note taking when . . .

My main goal for note taking is . . .

Action

The most important habit that I can adopt in order to meet my goal is . . .

By the time I finish this course, I would like my Notes score on the Discovery Wheel to be . . .

do you have a
MINUTE?

Take 60 seconds to convert a small section of your notes for one course into a different format. For example, take a paragraph of complete sentences and rewrite it as a concept map, mind map, or outline.

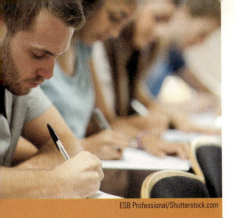

ESB Professional/Shutterstock.com

Maximizing Your Memory & Mastering Tests

why

Learning memory techniques can boost your skills at test taking—as well as reading, note taking, and many other tasks.

how

Think of a time when you struggled to remember something that was important. Perhaps you were trying to remember someone's name or recall some key information for a test. Then scan this chapter and find at least three strategies that you will use to prevent this problem in the future.

what if ...

I could let go of fear about tests—or anything else?

what is included ...

do you have a minute?

Write a study checklist for the next test in a course that you're taking right now. Include reading assignments and dates for class notes on which the test will be based.

Detach

This Power Process helps you release the powerful, natural student within you. It is especially useful whenever negative emotions are getting in your way.

Attachments are addictions. When we are attached to something, we think we cannot live without it, just as a drug addict feels he cannot live without drugs. We believe our well-being depends on maintaining our attachments.

We can be attached to just about anything: beliefs, emotions, people, roles, objects. The list is endless.

One person, for example, might be so attached to his car that he takes an accident as a personal attack. Pity the poor unfortunate who backs into this person's car. He might as well have backed into the owner himself.

Another person might be attached to her job. Her identity and sense of well-being depend on it. She could become depressed if she got fired.

When we are attached and things don't go our way, we can feel angry, sad, afraid, or confused.

Suppose you are attached to getting an A on your physics test. You feel as though your success in life depends on getting that A. As the clock ticks away, you work harder on the test, getting more stuck. That voice in your head gets louder: "I must get an A. I *must* get an A. *I must get an A!*"

Now is a time to detach. See whether you can just *observe* what's going on, letting go of all your judgments. When you observe rather than react, you reach a quiet state above and beyond your usual thoughts. This is a place where you can be aware of being aware. It's a tranquil spot, apart from your emotions. From here, you can see yourself objectively, as if you were watching someone else.

That place of detachment might sound far away and hard to reach. You can get there in three ways.

First, pay attention to your thoughts and physical sensations. If you are confused and feeling stuck, tell yourself, "Here I am, confused and stuck." If your palms are sweaty and your stomach is one big knot, admit it.

Second, practice relaxation. Start by simply noticing your breathing. Then breathe more slowly and more deeply. See whether you can breathe the relaxing feeling into your whole body.

Third, practice seeing current events from a broader perspective. In your mind, zoom out to a bigger picture. Ask yourself how much today's test score will matter to you in one week, one month, one year, or one decade from today. You can apply this technique to any challenge in life.

Caution: Giving up an *attachment* to being an A student does not mean giving up *being* an A student. Giving up an attachment to a job doesn't mean giving up the job. When you detach, you get to keep your values and goals. However, you know that you will be okay even if you fail to achieve a goal.

Remember that you are more than your goals. You are more than your thoughts and feelings. These things come and go. Meanwhile, the part of you that can *just observe* is always there and always safe, no matter what happens.

Behind your attachments is a master student. Release that mastery. Detach. ✖

GRADES:

The truth

On the surface, tests don't look dangerous. Yet sometimes we treat them as if they are land mines.

Imagine that a friend approached you in a coffee shop and asked, "Does a finite abelian P-group have a basis?" Would you break out in a cold sweat?

Probably not. Even if you had never heard of a finite abelian P-group, you're likely to remain cool and calm. However, if you find the same question on a test and you don't know anything about finite abelian P-groups, your hands might get clammy.

Tests become the object of fear and anxiety when we forget some basic facts about grades. For example:

- Grades are *not* a measure of your intelligence or creativity.
- Grades are *not* an indication of your ability to contribute to society.
- Grades are *not* a measure of your skills or your worth as a human being.
- Grades are *not* the only measure of what you accomplish in a course.

The truth is that a test score is simply a measure of what you scored on a test. If you are anxious about a test and blank out, the grade cannot measure what you've learned. The reverse is also true: If you are good at taking tests and you're a lucky guesser, the score won't be an accurate reflection of what you know.

Yet we tend to give test scores the power to determine how we feel about ourselves. Common thoughts include "If I fail a test, I am a failure" or "If I do badly on a test, I am a bad person."

If you do badly on a test, you are a person who did badly on a test. That's all. Even if you score low on an important test—such as an entrance test for college or medical school, bar exams, or CPA exams—this usually means only a delay.

If you experience test anxiety, then you might find this whole line of reasoning hard to swallow. Test anxiety is a common problem among students. It can surface in many ways, masquerading as a variety of emotions:

- *Anger:* "The teacher never wanted me to pass this stupid course anyway."
- *Blame:* "If only the class were not so boring."
- *Fear:* "I'll never have enough time to study."

Believing in any of these statements leaves us powerless. We become victims of things that we don't control—the teacher, the textbook, or the wording of the test questions.

Another option is to ask: "What can I do to experience my next test differently? How can I prepare more effectively? How can I manage stress before, during, and after the test?" When you answer such questions, you take back your power.

The key is to approach each test as a performance. From this point of view, preparing for a test means *rehearsing*. Study in the way that an actor prepares for a play—by simulating the conditions you'll encounter in the exam room. Do the kinds of tasks that you'll actually perform during a test: answering questions, solving problems, composing essays, and the like.

Carrying around misconceptions about tests and grades can put undue pressure on your performance. It's like balancing on a railroad track. Many people can walk along the rail and stay balanced for long periods. Yet the task seems entirely different if the rail is placed between two buildings, 52 stories up.

It is easier to do well on exams if you don't put too much pressure on yourself. Don't give the test some magical power over your own worth as a human being.

The way to deal with tests is to practice for them and keep your perspective. Keep the railroad track on the ground. ✕

BE READY

for your next test

When getting ready for tests, remember a key word—*review*. First create effective materials for review. Then use them often.

Corepics VOF/Shutterstock.com

Write review checklists. To begin your test preparation, make a list of what to review in each subject. Include items such as these:

- Reading assignments by chapters or page numbers
- Dates of lectures and major topics covered in each lecture
- Skills to master
- Key course content—definitions, theories, formulas, sample problems, and laboratory findings

A review checklist like Figure 5.1 is not a review sheet; it's a to-do list. These checklists contain the briefest possible description of each type of material that you intend to review. When you conduct your final review sessions, cross items off each checklist as you study them.

Create summary notes. Summary notes are materials that you create specifically to review for tests. They are separate from notes that you take throughout the term on lectures and readings. Summary notes tie together content from all sources—readings, lectures, handouts, lab sessions, and any other course elements.

AMERICAN HISTORY TEST

    Date: 11/1

    Materials:

— Lecture notes: 9/14–10/29

— Textbook, pages 190–323

— The Federalist, chapters 1, 2, 4, 6

    Topics:

— Hamilton and bank policies

— Frontier crisis

— Jay's treaty and foreign policy

Figure 5.1 **Sample Review Checklist**

You can create summary notes with a computer. Key in all your handwritten notes, and edit them into outline form. Or simply create an annotated table of contents for your handwritten notes. Note the date of each lecture, major topics, and main points. Even if you study largely from summary notes, keep the rest of your notes on file. They'll come in handy as backup sources of information.

Create flash cards. Flash cards are like portable test questions. Write them on 3×5 cards. On one side of the cards, write key terms or questions. On the other side, write definitions or answers. Buy an inexpensive card file, and arrange your flash cards by subject. Carry a pack of flash cards with you whenever you think you might have spare time to review. Keep a few blank cards with you to make flash cards as you recall new information.

You can also use apps to create flash cards, including with the accompanying MindTap (and MindTap for mobile) for this course. To discover additional options, search the Internet and your mobile app store for *flashcard apps.*

Whether you use cards or apps, take your review to a deep level. Don't stop when you've correctly answered each question just once. Shuffle your cards and answer them again in a different order. Make your answers more complete and precise. Repeat this process several times until you can recite answers accurately and easily.

Create a mock test. Make some predictions about what will be on the exam. Write your own exam questions, and take this "test" several times before the actual test. Design your mock test to look like the real thing. If possible, write out your answers in the room where the test will actually take place.

Plan your reviews. Take a little time each day to review your reading and lecture notes before and after class. This is a powerful tool for moving ideas from short-term to long-term memory.

Schedule time to review each subject once per week. Revisit assigned readings and lecture notes. Do something that forces you to rehearse the material. For example, look over any course summaries you've created and see whether you can re-create them from memory. Do the practice problems in your texts and answer end-of-chapter quiz questions.

In addition, make up questions of your own and answer those. Then compare your answers to your texts and class notes.

Also, schedule major reviews to do during the week before finals or other major exams. *To uncover gaps in knowledge, start major reviews at least three days before the test.*

During your reviews, alternate between courses. If you're studying for a math or science course, then review several formulas and practice solving several types of problems. Switching topics gives you more intense practice at recalling different types of information. In turn, this drives the information into your long-term memory.

In summary: Ask questions. Recite answers. Practice skills. Solve problems. Switch between subjects. Avoid passive techniques that put you to sleep, such as rereading texts and lecture notes for hours at a time. Stay awake, stay active, and switch it up. ⚑

As soon as an upcoming test is announced, take one minute to schedule a block of review time in your schedule. By committing well in advance, you're more likely to do it.

DISCOVERY / INTENTION STATEMENT

journal entry 6

Notice your excuses and let them go

Do a timed, four-minute brainstorm of all the reasons, rationalizations, justifications, and excuses you have used to avoid studying. Be creative. Write down your list of excuses.

Now, review your list. Then write a Discovery Statement about patterns that you see in your excuses.

I discovered that I . . .

Next, write an Intention Statement about what you will do to begin eliminating your favorite excuse.

I intend to . . .

12

memory techniques

Experiment with these techniques to develop a flexible, custom-made memory system that fits your style of learning.

1. Be selective. During your stay in higher education, you will be exposed to thousands of facts and ideas. No one expects you to memorize all of them. To a large degree, the art of memory is the art of selecting what to remember in the first place.

As you dig into your textbooks and notes, make choices about what is most important to learn. When reading, look for chapter previews, summaries, and review questions. Pay attention to anything printed in bold type. Also notice visual elements—tables, charts, graphs, and illustrations. They are all clues pointing to what's important. During lectures, notice what the instructor emphasizes. Anything that's presented visually—on the board, in overheads, or with slides—is probably key.

2. Review as soon as possible. A short review within minutes of a class or study session can move material from short-term memory into long-term memory. That quick mini-review—paired with a weekly review of all your class notes—can save you hours of study time when exams roll around.

3. Chunk it. Another way to move information into long-term memory is to break it down into smaller chunks. You already use this technique to dial phone numbers with an area code. For instance, 8006128030 gets chunked into several groups of numbers: 800-612-8030. Chunking works with many other types of information as well.

4. Recite. When you repeat something out loud, you anchor the concept in two different senses. First, you get the physical sensation in your throat, tongue, and lips when voicing the concept. Second, you hear it. The combined result is *synergistic*. That is, the effect of using two different senses is greater than the sum of their individual effects.

The "out loud" part is important. Reciting silently in your head can be useful—in the library, for example. Yet making noise can be even better. Your mind can trick itself into thinking it knows something when it doesn't. Your ears are harder to fool.

Don't forget to move your mouth. During a lecture, ask questions. Read key passages from textbooks out loud. Use a louder voice for the main points.

Recitation works better when you express concepts in your own words. For example, if you want to remember that, due to gravity, the acceleration of a falling body at sea level equals 32 feet per second per second, you might say, "At sea level, gravity makes an object accelerate 32 feet per second faster for each second that it's in the air." Putting a concept into your own words forces you to think about it.

Have some fun with this technique. Recite by writing a song about what you're learning. Sing it in the shower. Or imitate someone. Imagine your textbook being read by Ryan Reynolds or Lady Gaga.

5. Write it down. The technique of writing things down is obvious, yet easy to forget. Writing a note to yourself helps you remember an idea, even if you never look at the note again. Writing notes in the margins of your textbooks can help you remember what you read. You can extend this technique by writing down an idea not just once but many times.

Writing engages a different kind of memory than speaking. Writing prompts us to be more logical, coherent, and complete. Written reviews reveal gaps in knowledge that oral reviews miss, just as oral reviews reveal gaps that written reviews miss.

Finally, writing is physical. Your arm, your hand, and your fingers join in. Remember, learning is an active process—you remember what you *do*.

6. Create associations. The data already encoded in your neural networks are arranged according to a scheme that makes sense to you. When you introduce new data, you can remember them more effectively if you associate them with similar or related data.

Think about your favorite courses. They probably relate to subjects that you already know something about. If you have been interested in politics over the last few years, you'll probably find it easier to remember the facts in a modern history course.

To create associations, ask yourself questions about incoming information:

Does this remind me of something or someone I already know? Is this similar to a technique that I already use?

Even when you're tackling a new subject, you can build a mental store of basic background information—the raw material for creating associations. Preview reading assignments, and complete those readings before you attend lectures. Before taking upper-level courses, master the prerequisites.

7. Elaborate. *Elaboration* means asking questions to deepen your understanding. Creating associations is one way to elaborate.

Another way is to ask yourself questions such as these: *What are the key terms? What are the main ideas? Can I add examples of this concept from my own experience?*

You can also elaborate by connecting new information to your goals. You're more likely to remember material if it relates to something that evokes strong emotions. This is one reason why it pays to set goals and get specific about what you want. As you review your texts and class notes, ask: *How could I use this information to get something that matters to me?* To remember it, make it personal.

In addition, your brain thrives on finding contrasts between people, ideas, and things. Ask yourself: *How does this concept differ from what I already think? What's new about this procedure?*

If you're studying the concept of the unconscious mind in psychology, then ask how it differs from the conscious mind. If you want to understand the concept of inflation, then ask how it differs from deflation. Creating a simple two-column chart that lists the key features of each concept can help.

8. Use it. Many courses in higher education lean heavily toward abstract thinking. Create opportunities to actively experiment with ideas, and test them in daily life. For example, your introductory psychology book probably offers some theories about how people remember information. Choose one of those theories, and test it on yourself. See whether it helps you learn. Your sociology class might include a discussion about how groups of people resolve conflict. See whether you can apply any of those ideas to resolving conflict in your own life right now.

To remember an idea, go beyond thinking about it. Make it personal. *Do* something with it. Ask yourself if new information calls for long-term changes in your thinking and behavior. Then write goals and design habits to implement those changes.

9. Organize it. You remember things better if they have meaning for you. You can organize any list of items—even random items—in a way that makes them easier to remember. Although there are an infinite number of facts, there are only a finite number of ways to organize them.

One way to create meaning is to move from *general to specific*. Before you begin your next reading assignment, skim the passage to locate the main ideas. If you're ever lost, step back and look at the big picture. The details then might make more sense.

Another option is to organize any group of items by *category*. You can apply this suggestion to long to-do lists. For example, write each item on a separate index card. Then create a pile of cards for calls to make, errands to run, and household chores to complete. These will become your working categories.

The same concept applies to the content of your courses. In chemistry, a common example of organizing by category is the periodic table of chemical elements. When reading a novel for a literature course, you can organize your notes in categories such as theme, setting, and plot. Then take any of these categories and divide them into subcategories such as major events and minor events in the story.

Another option is to organize by *chronological order*. Any time that you create a numbered list of ideas, events, or steps, you are organizing by chronological order. To remember the events that led up to the stock market crash of 1929, for instance, create a time line. List the key events on index cards. Then arrange the cards by the date of each event.

You can also organize by *spatial order*. In plain English, this means making a map. When studying for a history exam, for example, you can create a rough map of the major locations where events take place.

Finally, there's an old standby for organizing lists—putting items in *alphabetical* order. It's simple. It works.

10. Create pictures. Draw diagrams. Make cartoons. Create images to connect facts and illustrate relationships. The key is to use your imagination. Creating pictures reinforces visual and kinesthetic learning styles.

For example, Boyle's law states that at a constant temperature the volume of a confined ideal gas varies inversely with its pressure. Simply put, cutting the volume in half doubles the pressure. To remember this concept, you might picture someone "doubled over," using a bicycle pump. As she increases the pressure in the pump by decreasing the volume in the pump cylinder, she seems to be getting angrier. By the time she has doubled the pressure (and halved the volume), she is boiling ("Boyle-ing") mad.

Another reason to create pictures is that visual information is associated with a part of the brain that is different from the part that processes verbal information. When you create a picture of a concept, you are anchoring the information in a second part of your brain. Doing so increases your chances of recalling that information.

To visualize abstract relationships effectively, create an action-oriented image, such as the person using the pump. Make the picture vivid too. The person's face could be bright red. And involve all of your senses. Imagine how the cold metal of the pump would feel and how the person would grunt as she struggled with it.

3/19/03
U.S. inva...
Iraq

Figure 5.2

You car...
study by u...
visual meth...
tion can he...
among fac...

Someti...
to rememb...
story or his...
line by dra...
points in o...
key events...
the left en...
toward the...
start of a ti...
the U.S. wa...

When y...
contrast tw...
kind of gra...
diagram. R...
circle. Dra...
overlap. In...
characteris...
share. In th...
list the uni...
thing. Figu...
types of jo...
this text—...
Intention ...

Discovery

Figure 5.3

MATH
essentials

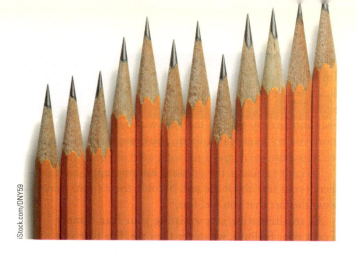

iStock.com/DNY59

Many students who could succeed in math shy away from the subject. Some had negative experiences in past courses. Others believe that math is only for gifted students.

At some level, however, math is open to all students. There's more to this subject than memorizing formulas and manipulating numbers. Imagination, creativity, and problem-solving skills are important too.

Consider a three-part program for math success. Begin with strategies for overcoming math anxiety. Next, boost your study skills. Finally, let your knowledge shine during tests.

OVERCOME MATH ANXIETY

Many schools offer courses in overcoming math anxiety. Ask your advisor about resources on your campus. Also experiment with the following suggestions.

Notice your mental pictures about math. Sometimes what keeps people from succeeding at math is their mental picture of mathematicians. They see a man dressed in a baggy plaid shirt and brown wingtip shoes. He's got a calculator on his belt and six pencils jammed in his shirt pocket.

These pictures are far from realistic. Succeeding in math won't turn you into a nerd. Actually, you'll be able to enjoy school more, and your friends will still like you.

Mental pictures about math can be funny, but they can have serious effects. If math is seen as a field for white males, then women and people of color are likely to get excluded. Promoting math success for all students helps overcome racism and sexism.

Change your conversation about math. When students fear math, they often say negative things to themselves about their abilities in this subject. Many times this self-talk includes statements such as *I'll never be fast enough at solving math problems* or *I'm good with words, so I can't be good with numbers.*

Get such statements out in the open, and apply some emergency critical thinking. You'll find two self-defeating assumptions lurking there: *Everybody else is better at math and science than I am* and *Because I don't understand a math concept right now, I'll never understand it.* Both of these statements are illogical.

Replace negative beliefs with logical, realistic statements that affirm your ability to succeed in math: *Any confusion I feel now can be resolved. I learn math without comparing myself to others.* And *I ask whatever questions are needed to aid my understanding.*

Connect math to life. Think of the benefits of mastering math courses. You'll have more options for choosing a major and a career. Math skills can also put you at ease in everyday situations—calculating the tip for a waiter, balancing your checkbook, working with a spreadsheet on a computer. If you follow baseball statistics, cook, do construction work, or snap pictures with a camera, you'll use math. And speaking the language of math can help you feel at home in a world driven by technology.

Remember that math is cumulative. This means that concepts build upon each other in a certain order. If you struggled with algebra, you may have trouble with trigonometry or calculus. To ensure that you have an adequate base of knowledge, tell the truth about your current level of knowledge and skill.

Before you register for a math course, locate assigned texts for the prerequisite courses. If the material in those books seems new or difficult for you, see the instructor. Ask for suggestions on ways to prepare for the course.

BOOST STUDY SKILLS FOR MATH

Choose teachers with care. Whenever possible, find a math teacher whose approach to math matches your learning style. Talk with several teachers until you find one you enjoy.

In some cases, only one teacher will be offering the math course you need. The suggestions that follow can be used to learn from a teacher regardless of her teaching style.

Take math courses back to back. Approach math in the same way that you learn a foreign language. If you take a year off in between Spanish I and Spanish II, you won't gain much fluency. To master a language, you take courses back to back. It works the same way with math, which is a language in itself.

Avoid short courses. Courses that you take during summer school or another shortened term are condensed. You might find yourself doing far more reading and homework each week than you do in longer courses. If you enjoy math, the extra intensity can provide a stimulus to learn. If math is not your favorite subject, then give yourself extra time. Enroll in courses spread out over more calendar days.

Form a study group. During the first week of each math course, organize a study group. Ask each member to bring five problems to group meetings, along with solutions. Also exchange contact information so that you can stay in touch via e-mail, phone, and text messaging.

Make your text top priority. Math courses are often text driven. Budget for math textbooks, and buy them as early as possible. Class activities closely follow the book. This fact underscores the importance of completing your reading assignments. Master one concept before going on to the next, and stay current with your reading. Be willing to read slowly, and reread sections as needed.

Do homework consistently. Students who succeed in math do their homework daily—from beginning to end, and from the easy problems all the way through the hard problems. If you do homework consistently, you're not likely to be surprised on a test.

Take notes that promote success in math. Though math courses are often text driven, you might find that the content and organization of your notes make a big difference as well.

Take notes during every class, and organize them by date. Also, number the pages of your notes. Create a table of contents or index for them, so you can locate key concepts quickly.

Participate in class. Success in math depends on your active involvement. Attend class regularly. Complete homework assignments *when they're due*—not just before the test. If you're confused, get help right away from an instructor, tutor, or study group. Instructors' office hours, free on-campus tutoring, and classmates are just a few of the resources available to you. Also support class participation with time for homework. Make daily contact with math.

Ask questions fearlessly. It's a cliché, and it's true: In math, there are no dumb questions. Ask whatever questions will aid your understanding. Keep a running list of them, and bring the list to class.

Read actively. To get the most out of your math texts, read with paper and pencil in hand. Work out examples. Copy diagrams, formulas, and equations. Use chapter summaries and introductory outlines to organize your learning. From time to time, stop, close your book, and mentally reconstruct the steps in solving a problem. Before you memorize a formula, understand the basic concepts behind it.

USE TESTS TO SHOW WHAT YOU KNOW

Practice problem solving. To get ready for math tests, work *lots* of problems. Find out whether practice problems or previous tests are on file in the library, in the math department, or with your math teacher.

Isolate the types of problems that you find the most difficult. Practice them more often. Be sure to get help with these kinds of problems *before* exhaustion or frustration sets in.

To prepare for tests, practice working problems fast. Time yourself. This activity is a great one for math study groups.

Practice test taking. In addition to solving problems, create practice tests:

- Print out a set of problems, and set a timer for the same length of time as your testing period.
- Whenever possible, work on these problems in the same room where you will take the actual test.
- Use only the kinds of supporting materials—such as scratch paper or lists of formulas—that will be allowed during the test.
- As you work problems, use deep breathing or another technique to enter a more relaxed state.

To get the most value from practice tests, use them to supplement—not replace—your daily homework.

Ask appropriate questions. If you don't understand a test item, ask for clarification. The worst that can happen is that an instructor or proctor will politely decline to answer your question.

Write legibly. Put yourself in the instructor's place. Imagine the prospect of grading stacks of illegible answer sheets. Make your answers easy to read. If you show your work, underline key sections, and circle your answer.

Do your best. There are no secrets involved in getting ready for math tests. Master some stress-management techniques, do your homework, get answers to your questions, and work sample problems. If you've done those things, you're ready for the test and deserve to do well. If you haven't done all those things, just do the best you can.

Remember that your personal best can vary from test to test, and even from day to day. Even if you don't answer all test questions correctly, you can demonstrate what you *do* know right now.

During the test, notice when solutions come easily. Savor the times when you feel relaxed and confident. If you ever feel math anxiety in the future, these are the times to remember.[1]

Take a minute to reflect on your responses to the "Memory & Tests" section of the Discovery Wheel. Then take your discoveries and intentions about tests to the next level by completing the following sentences:

Discovery

My score on the Memory & Tests section of the Discovery Wheel was . . .

To study for a test, what I usually do is to . . .

Intention

By the time I finish this course, I would like my Memory & Tests score on the Discovery Wheel to be . . .

For now, my main goal related to memory and test taking is . . .

Action

To reach my goal, the next habit that I will adopt is . . .

Review the action statement that you just wrote. Make sure that you include a clear trigger (cue) that will remind you to do this new behavior. Also describe how you intend to reward yourself for practicing this habit. Keep it simple, like doing a fist pump or saying *Yes!* to yourself.

chapter 6

La1n/Shutterstock.com

Developing Information Literacy

why

Succeeding in school and the workplace depends on managing and making sense of continuous streams of information from many sources, both online and offline.

how

Think of a time when you wanted to research a topic but felt lost about how to begin—or about how to evaluate the information that you already had on hand. Then scan this chapter for at least three strategies you can use to prevent such problems in the future.

what if...

I could immediately find the exact information that I need for any purpose—from creating a presentation or writing a paper to solving a problem or completing a project at work?

what is included...

do you have a minute?

In just 60 seconds, you can take simple actions to become more efficient at managing information. For example:

- Make a list of all the ways that digital information enters your life—through email, voicemail, text messages, online newspapers, and social media websites, and "apps" on a laptop computer or mobile phone.
- Review this list of digital "inboxes" and look for one that you can eliminate.
- Find an email that's been sitting in your inbox for a long time. Choose whether to respond to it, archive it, or delete it.

WebCrawler (**www.webcrawler.com**), and Info.com (**http://info.com**). For a more complete list of metasearch engines, go online to **www.pandia.com/articles/metasearch**.

Some deep websites often have their own search engines, such as:

- H. W. Wilson (www.hwwilson.com)
- Highbeam Research (www.highbeam.com)
- NewsBank (www.newsbank.com)
- Wolters Kluwer UpToDate (www.uptodate.com)
- Gale (www.gale.com)

To find more deep Web sources, go to your school library and talk to a librarian.

VISIT THE LIBRARY

Remember that many published materials are available in print as well as online. This is another reason to visit a library. Start by talking to a reference librarian. Tell this person about the questions you want to answer, and ask for good sources of information. Also visit your library's website.

Remember that libraries—from the smallest one in your hometown to the Smithsonian in Washington, D.C.—consist of just three basic elements:

- **Catalogs**—databases that list all of the library's accessible sources.
- **Collections**—materials, such as periodicals (magazines, journals, and newspapers), books, pamphlets, ebooks, audiobooks, and materials available from other libraries via interlibrary loan.
- **Online resources**—Internet databases that allow you to look at full-text articles from magazines, journals, and newspapers.

Ask a librarian for help with finding online resources. Many of these are focused on specific subjects. For example, the ERIC database (**www.eric.ed.gov**) is an index of publications by and for professional educators. The National Library of Medicine (**www.nlm.nih.gov**) focuses on medical research. And for psychologists there is PsycINFO® from the American Psychological Association (**www.apa.org/psychinfo**).

TALK TO PEOPLE

Making direct contact with people can offer a welcome relief from hours of solitary research and give you valuable hands-on involvement. Your initial research will uncover the names of experts on your chosen topic. Consider doing an interview with one of these people—in person, over the phone, or via email.

To get the most from interviews:

- Schedule a specific time and place for the interview—if you're meeting the expert in person. Agree on the length of the interview in advance and work within that time frame.
- Enter the interview with a short list of questions to ask. Allow time for additional questions that occur to you during the interview.
- If you want to record the interview, ask for permission in advance. When talking to people who don't want to be recorded, be prepared to take handwritten notes.
- Ask experts for permission to quote their comments.
- Be courteous before, during, and after the interview. Thank the person for taking time to talk with you.
- End the interview at your agreed-on time.
- Follow up on the interview with a thank-you note.
- Be sure to cite your interview as a source for your research. ✄

do you have a
MINUTE?

Go online to your school's website. Look for a link to the campus library and a list of its services. Then, on the library's website, look for a page with a title such as "Research Help" or "Get Help—Ask a Librarian."

INFORMATION:

Reflecting on it

Your job doesn't end after you have collected your information: you need to dig in to the merits of it.

After finding answers to the questions that started your research, take some time away from it—at least one day. Do some things that are totally unrelated to your research project. The goal is to get some distance from all information you gathered. Then you can return to it with a clear head and fresh perspective.

THINK CRITICALLY

After doing in-depth research, do you have any lingering questions about your topic? Would the answers that you currently have satisfy a reader or listener who belongs to your intended audience? If not, go back and do some more research.

Critical thinking is crucial at this stage. Some students assume that anything that's published in print or online is true. Unfortunately, that's not the case. Some sources of information are more reliable than others. In fact, some websites are simply "click bait"—filled with misleading claims or outright falsehoods that are meant to grab your attention and generate advertising revenue.

To evaluate your sources of information, look for the following:

- **Publication date.** If your topic is time-sensitive, then set some guidelines about how current you want your sources to be—for example, that they were published during the last five years.
- **Credibility.** Scan the source for biographical information about the author. Look for educational degrees, training, and work experience that qualify this person to publish on the topic of your research.
- **Bias.** Determine what the website or other source is "selling"—the product, service, or point of view it promotes. Political affiliations or funding sources might color the author's point of view. For instance, you can predict that a pamphlet on gun control policies that's printed with funding from the National Rifle Association will promote certain points of view. Round out your research with other sources on the topic.

  Evaluate Internet sources with extra care. Ask the following questions:
- **Who pays for the site?** Carefully check information from any organization that sells advertising. Look for an "About This Site" link—a clue to sources of funding. Avoid sources with content that's controlled by advertisers or sponsors.
- **Who runs the site?** Look for a clear description of the person or organization responsible for the content. If the sponsoring person or organization did not create the site's content, then find out who did.

- **How is the site's content selected?** Look for a link that lists members of an editorial board or other qualified reviewers.
- **Does the site support claims with evidence?** Credible sites base their editorial stands on expert opinion and facts from scientific studies. If you find grandiose claims supported only by testimonials, beware. When something sounds too good to be true, it probably is.
- **How can readers connect with the site?** Look for a way to contact the site's publisher with questions and comments. See whether you can find a physical address, email address, and phone number. Sites that conceal this information might conceal other facts. Also inspect reader comments on the site to see whether a variety of opinions are allowed.
- **Does the site link to other sites?** Think critically about these sites as well.

Many websites from government agencies, educational institutions, and nonprofit organizations have strict and clearly stated editorial policies. These sites are often good places to start your research.

THINK CREATIVELY

Here's where the "aha!" happens. Make time to digest all the information you've gathered and look for patterns. The whole art of creative thinking is to see fresh connections between ideas. Ask yourself:

- Do I have answers to my main question?
- Do I have answers to my supporting questions?
- How do my sources answer these questions?
- Do I have personal experiences that can also help me answer these questions?
- On what points do my sources agree?
- On what points do my sources disagree?
- Can I take the problems raised by my sources and state them in a different way?
- Can I offer new solutions—or modify and combine existing solutions?
- Do I have facts and examples that I can use to support my conclusions and solutions?

The beauty of these questions is that they stimulate *your* thinking. The result can be a powerful paper, presentation, or other carefully crafted message that you're proud to share with the world. ⚔

Discover the impact of technology on your time and attention

In 2008, Nicholas Carr published a widely quoted article: "Is Google Making Us Stupid?"[1] In it, he complained that his Web-surfing habits were chipping away at his ability to concentrate and read for long periods of time. "Once I was a scuba diver in the sea of words," Carr wrote. "Now I zip along the surface like a guy on a Jet Ski."

No single website has the power to make us stupid. Yet the habits that we develop while we're online might affect our ability to "be here now." This issue presents a perfect opportunity to apply the cycle of discovery, intention, and action.

Discovery

Begin by keeping track of the time that you spend online. Do this for at least one day—or better yet, a full week.

Use a simple system for gathering data. For instance, keep a 3 × 5 card and pen in your pocket or purse. On this card, write down the times when you start using the Internet and when you stop. Another option is to use a Web-based time tracker such as SlimTimer (**slimtimer.com**) or Rescuetime (**rescuetime.com**). Or simply estimate your online time at the end of each day.

If possible, add short descriptions of how you spend your blocks of online time. For example: *visit Facebook, check email, read the news, do course work, or watch videos.*

After monitoring your online time, complete the following sentences:

I discovered that the average number of minutes I spend online during the day is . . .

The most common things that I do online are . . .

I was surprised to discover that . . .

Intention

Next, think about any changes that you want to make in the amount of time you spend online—and the ways you use that time. For example, you could:

- Turn off all notifications for email messages, social networking updates, and text messages while you study.
- Close your Web browser for defined periods each day.
- Check your email only at specific times each day.
- Stay offline entirely during certain times of the day, or on certain days of the week.

Think about the strategies you'd like to use. Then choose one of them to use during the upcoming week. Complete the following sentence:

I intend to . . .

Action

After acting on your intention for one week, come back to this Journal Entry. Reflect on the results of your new habit.

During the past week of online activity, I spent less time on . . .

I spent more time on . . .

The most important thing I can do right now to take charge of time and attention while online is to . . .

Review your responses to the Information Literacy section of the Discovery Wheel. Then plan to take your skills in this area to the next level by completing the following sentences.

Discovery

My score on the Information Literacy section of the Discovery Wheel was . . .

Right now, my biggest challenge in developing information literacy is . . .

I'll know that I've overcome this challenge when I am able to . . .

Intention

By the time I finish this course, I intend for my score on the Information Literacy section of the Discovery Wheel to be . . .

To overcome my biggest challenge in developing information literacy, I will . . .

Action

To act on my intentions, I will adopt the following habits:

do you have a
MINUTE?

One aim of this text is to help you discover the power in short bursts of focused activity. Review the habits you intend to adopt in order to develop information literacy. Have you stated these habits as actions that you can start taking immediately? If not, then take a minute to rewrite your intention statements now:

Nestor Rizhniak/Shutterstock.com

Thinking Critically & Communicating Your Ideas

why

Your skills in thinking, writing, and speaking have a direct impact on your success in school and at work.

how

Remember a time in your life when you struggled to make a decision, solve a problem, or finish a writing assignment. Then scan this chapter to find useful suggestions for completing these tasks in the future.

what if ...

I could make effective decisions, solve problems, and consistently persuade people to adopt my ideas?

what is included ...

do you have a minute?

Writing a paper or speech doesn't have to mean pulling an all-nighter just before the due date. Start now! In just 60 seconds you can:

- Brainstorm a list of topics for a paper.
- Brainstorm a list of questions about your topic.
- Enter one of those questions into a search engine.

Embrace the new

Heraclitus, the ancient Greek philosopher, said that you can never step into the same river twice. A river is dynamic—ever flowing, ever changing.

The same thing is true of you.

Right now, you are not the same person you were when you started reading this page. Nerve cells in your brain are firing messages and making connections that didn't exist a second ago. There is new breath in your lungs. Old cells in your body have been replaced by new ones.

What's true about your body is also true of your behavior. Think about all the activities that depend on embracing the new: going to school, gaining knowledge, acquiring skills, succeeding with technology, making friends, and falling in love.

Both creative thinking and critical thinking call on us to embrace the new. We can think critically about a new idea only if we're willing to *consider* it in the first place. And it's hard to create something original or change our behavior if we insist on sticking with what's already familiar to us. All the game-changing devices in human history—from the wheel to the iPhone—happened only because their inventors were willing to embrace the new.

Embracing the new is more than just a nice idea. It's an essential skill for anyone who wants to survive and thrive in the work world. Your next career might be one that doesn't exist today. Think about certain job titles—*information architect, social media director, content strategist*—that came to life only in the twenty-first century. There are many more opportunities just waiting to be created.

When learning to embrace the new, start with the way you speak. Notice comments such as these:

"That can't possibly be true."

"That idea will never work."

"We tried that last year and failed."

Those statements represent the sound of a closed mind snapping shut. Consider replacing them with:

"What if that *were* true?"

"How could we make that idea work?"

"What could we do differently this time?"

To get the most value from this suggestion, remember that it's about more than being open to ideas. You can embrace the new on many levels: be willing to think what you've never thought before, to say what you've never said before, to do what you've never done before. This is the essence of learning, and it's the heart of this text.

Also remember that embracing the new does *not* mean trashing the old. Adopting a new attitude does not mean giving up all your current attitudes. Adopting a new habit does not mean changing all your current habits. When you open up to unfamiliar ideas and experiences, you get to keep your core values. You can embrace change and still take a stand for what's important to you.

As you test new ideas and experiment with new strategies, keep those that work and let go of the rest. You might find that your current beliefs and behaviors work well with just a few tweaks and subtle changes. And in any case, you can go into the unknown with a known process—the cycle of discovery, intention, and action.

What's new is often going to stick around anyway. You have two basic options: resist it or embrace it. The former is a recipe for frustration. The latter offers a fresh possibility in every moment. ✕

Critical thinking:
A SURVIVAL SKILL

Society depends on persuasion. Advertisers want us to spend money on their products. Political candidates want us to "buy" their stands on the issues. Teachers want us to agree that their classes are vital to our success. Parents want us to accept their values. Authors want us to read their books. And broadcasters want us to spend our time in front of the radio or television, consuming their programs instead of those from the competition.

A typical American sees thousands of television commercials each year—and TV is just one medium of communication. There are also writers and speakers who enter our lives through radio shows, magazines, books, billboards, brochures, websites, and fund-raising appeals. They all have a product, service, cause, or opinion for us to embrace.

This flood of appeals leaves us with hundreds of choices about what to buy, what to do, and who to be. It's easy to lose our heads in the crosscurrent of competing ideas—unless we develop skills in critical thinking.

When we think critically, we make choices with open eyes. We detect thinking that's inaccurate, sloppy, or misleading. We embrace critical thinking as a path to freedom from half-truths and deception. This is liberating.

Critical thinking is a skill that will never go out of style. One reason is that people have a remarkable capacity to fool themselves. Throughout human history, nonsense has often been taken for the truth. For example, people once believed that:

- Illness results from an imbalance in the four vital fluids: blood, phlegm, water, and bile.
- Racial integration of the armed forces will lead to destruction of soldiers' morale.
- Women are incapable of voting intelligently.
- We will never invent anything smaller than a transistor. (That was before the computer chip.)

The critical thinkers of history arose to challenge such ideas. Those courageous men and women were master students. They held their peers to high intellectual standards.

It's been said that human beings are rational creatures. Yet no one is born as a creative or critical thinker. These are learned skills.

This is one reason that you study so many subjects in higher education—math, science, history, psychology, literature, and more. A broad base of courses helps you develop as a thinker. You see how people with different viewpoints arrive at conclusions, make decisions, and solve problems. You get a foundation for dealing with complex challenges in your career, your relationships, and your community.

When thinking critically, we see that some ill-formed thoughts and half-truths have a source that hits a little close to home. That source is ourselves.

If they discover that their thinking is fuzzy, lazy, based on a false assumption, or dishonest, master students are willing to admit the truth. These students value evidence and logic. When a solid fact contradicts a cherished belief, such students are willing to change the belief.

Thinking, both critical and creative, is the basis for everything you do in school—reading, writing, speaking, listening, note taking, test taking, problem solving, and decision making. Master students have strategies for accomplishing all these tasks. These students distinguish between opinion and fact. They ask probing questions and make detailed observations. They uncover assumptions and define their terms. They state opinions carefully, basing them on sound logic and solid evidence. Almost everything that we call *knowledge* is a result of these activities. Thinking and learning are intimately linked.

You have the right to question everything that you see, hear, and read. You also have the opportunity to *create* new ideas that can transform your life and contribute to the lives of others. Acquiring these abilities is a major goal of education.

Use the suggestions in this chapter to claim the thinking powers that are your birthright. The effective thinker is one aspect of the master student who lives inside you. ✄

do you have a MINUTE?

The statement *We tried that idea before, and it didn't work* can shut down creative thinking. To replace this statement, take a minute to pose a more creative question. One possibility is *What can we do differently this time?*

Becoming a critical
THINKER

Although there are many possible approaches to thinking well, the process boils down to *asking and answering questions*. This is one place where master students shine. They know ways to ask questions that lead to deeper learning.

Remember that your mind is an obedient servant. It will deliver answers at the same level as your questions. Becoming a critical thinker means staying flexible and asking a wide range of questions.

You can use a set of questions based on the six levels of thinking described by psychologist Benjamin Bloom (see Figure 7.1):[1]

- Remembering
- Understanding
- Applying
- Analyzing
- Evaluating
- Creating

All levels of thinking are useful, and they differ. For example, the lower levels of thinking (1 to 3) give you fewer options than the higher levels (4 to 6). Lower levels of thinking are sometimes about finding one "right" answer to a question. At levels 5 and 6, you can discover several valid answers and create your own solutions. These

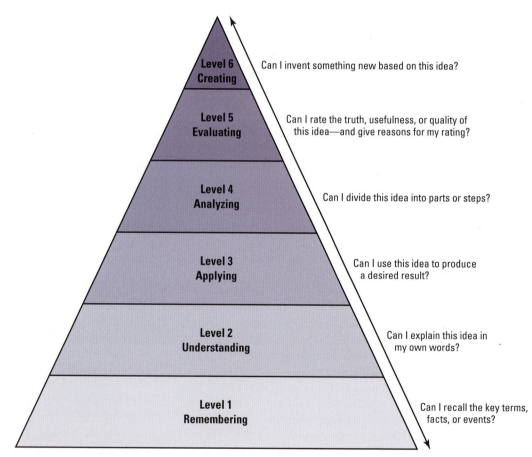

Level 6 Creating — Can I invent something new based on this idea?

Level 5 Evaluating — Can I rate the truth, usefulness, or quality of this idea—and give reasons for my rating?

Level 4 Analyzing — Can I divide this idea into parts or steps?

Level 3 Applying — Can I use this idea to produce a desired result?

Level 2 Understanding — Can I explain this idea in my own words?

Level 1 Remembering — Can I recall the key terms, facts, or events?

Figure 7.1 **Bloom's Taxonomy**

are signs of mastery in the realms of critical and creative thinking. Following are strategies that you can use to move freely through all six levels of thinking.

CHECK YOUR ATTITUDES

Be willing to find various points of view on any issue. Imagine George Bush, Cesar Chavez, and Barack Obama assembled in one room to debate the most desirable way to reshape our government. Picture Madonna, Oprah Winfrey, and Mark Zuckerberg leading a workshop on how to plan your career. When seeking out alternative points of view, let scenes like these unfold in your mind.

Dozens of viewpoints exist on every important issue—reducing crime, ending world hunger, preventing war, educating our children, and countless other concerns. In fact, few problems have any single, permanent solution. Each generation produces its own answers to critical questions, based on current conditions. Our search for answers is a conversation that spans centuries. On each question, many voices are waiting to be heard. Add yours to the mix.

You can begin by seeking out alternative views, keeping an open mind. When talking to another person, be willing to walk away with a new point of view—even if it's the one you brought to the table, supported with new evidence.

When asking questions, let go of the temptation to settle for just a single answer. Look for at least three. This is especially important when you're *sure* that you have the right answer to a complex question. Once you come up with a new possibility, say to yourself, "Yes, that is one answer. Now what's another?" Using this approach can lead to honest inquiry, creativity, and breakthroughs.

Be prepared: The world is complicated, and critical thinking is a complex business. Some of your answers might contradict others. Resist the temptation to have all of your ideas in a neat, orderly bundle.

Practice tolerance. One path to critical thinking is tolerance for a wide range of opinions. Taking a position on important issues is natural. When we stop having an opinion on things, we've probably stopped breathing.

Problems occur when we become so attached to our current viewpoints that we refuse to consider alternatives. Likewise, it can be disastrous when we blindly follow everything any person or group believes, without questioning its validity.

Many ideas that are widely accepted in Western cultures—for example, civil liberties for people of color and the right of women to vote—were once considered dangerous. Viewpoints that seem outlandish today might become widely accepted a century, a decade, or even a year from now. Remembering this idea can help us practice tolerance for differing beliefs. Doing this makes room for new ideas that can transform our lives.

Understand before criticizing. Notice that the six levels of thinking build on each other. Before you agree or disagree with an idea, make sure that you *remember* it accurately and truly *understand* it. Polished debaters make a habit of doing this. Often they can sum up their opponents' viewpoint better than anyone else can. This put them in a much stronger position to *apply, analyze, evaluate,* and *create* ideas.

Effective understanding calls for reading and listening while suspending judgment. Enter another person's world by expressing her viewpoint in your own words. If you're conversing with that person, keep revising your summary until she agrees that you've stated her position accurately. If you're reading an article, write a short summary of it. Then scan the article again, checking to see whether your synopsis is on target.

Watch for "hot spots." Many people have mental "hot spots"—topics that provoke strong opinions and feelings. Examples are abortion, homosexuality, gun control, and the death penalty.

To become more skilled at examining various points of view, notice your own particular hot spots. Make a clear intention to accept your feelings about these topics and to continue using critical thinking techniques in relation to them.

Be willing to be uncertain. Some of the most profound thinkers have practiced the art of thinking by using a magic sentence: "I'm not sure yet." Take the time to pause, to look, to examine, to be thoughtful, to consider many points of view—and to be unsure.

CHECK FOR LOGIC

Logic is a branch of philosophy that seeks to distinguish between valid and invalid reasoning. Students of logic look at a series of related sentences to make sure that they are clear, consistent, and coherent.

Learning to think logically offers many benefits: When you think logically, you take your reading, writing, speaking, and listening skills to a higher level. You avoid costly mistakes in decision making. You can join discussions and debates with more confidence, cast your election votes with a clear head, and become a better-informed citizen.

The following suggestions will help you work with the building blocks of logical thinking—terms, assertions, arguments, assumptions.

Define key terms. A *term* is a word or phrase that refers to a clearly defined concept. Terms with several different meanings are ambiguous—fuzzy, vague, and unclear. One common goal of critical thinking is to remove ambiguous terms or define them clearly.

Conflicts of opinion can often be resolved—or at least clarified—when we define our key terms up front. This is especially true with abstract, emotion-laden terms such as *freedom, peace, progress,* or *justice*. Blood has been shed over the meaning of those words. Define them with care.

Your first task is to locate key terms. Skilled writers and speakers often draw attention to them. Even when they don't, you can use clues to spot them:

- Look or listen for words that are new to you.
- Be alert for words or phrases that are frequently repeated—especially in prominent places in a text or in a speech, such as an overview, introduction, summary, or conclusion.
- When reading, check the index for words or phrases that have many page references.

Also see whether the text includes a glossary. And look for words that are printed in *italics* or **boldface**.

As you look for clues, remember that several different words or phrases can stand for the same term. In this chapter, for example, *self-evident truth* and *assumption* are different words that refer to the same concept.

Look for assertions. A speaker or writer's key terms occur in a larger context called an assertion. An *assertion* is a complete sentence that contains one or more key terms. The purpose of an assertion is to define a term or to state relationships between terms. These relationships are the essence of what we mean by the term *knowledge*.

To find a speaker or writer's assertions, listen or look for key sentences. These are sentences that make an important point or state a general conclusion.

Often speakers and writers will give you clues to their key sentences. Speakers will pause to emphasize these sentences or precede them with phrases such as "My point is that...." Writers may present key sentences in italics or boldface, or include them in summaries.

Look for arguments. Most of us think of an argument as the process of disagreement or conflict. For specialists

in logic, this term has a different meaning. For them, an *argument* is a series of related assertions.

There are two major types of reasoning used in building arguments—deductive and inductive.

Deductive reasoning builds arguments by starting with a general assertion and leading to a more specific one. Here's a classic example that you might hear in a beginning philosophy course. It involves Socrates, an ancient Greek philosopher:

- All men are mortal.
- Socrates is a man.
- Therefore, Socrates is mortal.

These three assertions make an argument that Socrates is mortal. Notice that in deductive reasoning, each assertion is like a link in a chain. A weakness or error in any link can break the entire chain.

With *inductive reasoning*, the chain of logic proceeds in the opposite direction—from specific to general. Suppose that you apply for a job and the interviewer says, "We hired two people from your school who did not work out well for us. When we found out where you're taking classes, our management team was concerned."

In this case, the interviewer began with specific examples ("We hired two people from your school"). From there he proceeded to a more general conclusion, which went unstated: *Therefore, students from your school do not make good employees.* This argument is a simple example of inductive reasoning.

As you can see, inductive reasoning can also contain errors. One is the error of *hasty generalization*—coming to a conclusion too quickly. For example, experience with two graduates does not offer enough evidence for judging the abilities of hundreds, or even thousands, of people who get degrees from your school.

Another possible error is the *false cause*. You will often observe one event that usually happens after

another event. However, this does not mean that the first event *caused* the second event. It's true, for example, that children get more dental cavities as they develop a larger vocabulary. However, this does not mean that a large vocabulary causes cavities. Rather, a third factor is involved: children learn more words *and* get more cavities as they get older. Age is the key factor—not vocabulary.

Look for unstated assumptions. In many cases, assumptions are unstated and offered without evidence. They can sneak up on you in the middle of an argument and take you on a one-way trip to confusion.

In addition, people often hold many assumptions at the same time. And those assumptions might contradict each other. This makes uncovering assumptions a feat worthy of the greatest detective.

You can follow a two-step method for testing the validity of any argument. First, state the assumptions. Second, see whether you can find any exceptions to the assumptions.

Consider this statement: "My mother and father have a good marriage—after all, they're still together after 35 years." Behind this statement is an assumption: *If you've been married a long time, you must have a good relationship.* Yet there are possible exceptions. You might know married couples who have stayed together for decades, even though are unhappy in the relationship.

Uncovering assumptions and looking for exceptions can help you detect many errors in logic. This is a tool you can pull out any time you want to experience the benefits of critical thinking.

CHECK FOR EVIDENCE
In addition to testing arguments with the tools of logic, look carefully at the evidence used to support those arguments. Evidence comes in several forms, including facts, comments from recognized experts in a field, and examples.

To think critically about evidence, ask the following questions:

- Are all or most of the relevant facts presented?
- Are the facts consistent with each other?
- Are facts presented accurately?
- Are enough examples included to make a solid case for the assertion?
- Do the examples truly support the assertion?
- Are the examples typical? That is, could the author or speaker support the assertion with other examples that are similar?
- Is the expert credible—truly knowledgeable about the topic?
- Is the expert biased? For example, is the expert paid to represent the views of a corporation that is promoting a product or service?
- Is the expert quoted accurately?
- If the speaker or writer appeals to your emotions, is this done in a way that is also logical and based on evidence?

Answering these questions takes time and intellectual energy. It's worth it. You'll gain skills in critical thinking that will help you succeed in any class or career that you choose. ✴

do you have a
MINUTE?

Use Bloom's Taxonomy when you review class notes to predict a possible test question.

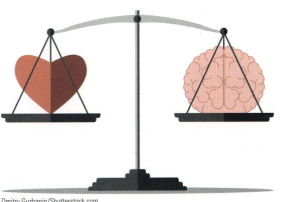

Dmitry Guzhanin/Shutterstock.com

Over the last few thousand years, philosophers have listed some classic land mines in the field of logic. These common mistakes in thinking are called *fallacies*. The study of fallacies could fill a year-long course. Following are some examples to get you started. Knowing about them can help you avoid getting fooled.

JUMPING TO CONCLUSIONS

Jumping to conclusions is the only exercise that some lazy thinkers get. This fallacy involves drawing conclusions without sufficient evidence.

Don't fool yourself: Common mistakes in LOGIC

Consider the bank officer who hears about a student's failing to pay back an education loan. After that, the officer turns down all loan applications from students. This person has formed a rigid opinion on the basis of hearsay. Jumping to conclusions—also called *hasty generalization*—is at work here. Following are more examples of this fallacy:

- When I went to Mexico for spring break, I felt sick the whole time. Mexican food makes people sick.
- Google's mission is to "organize the world's information." Their employees must be on a real power trip.
- During a recession, more people go to the movies. People just want to sit in the dark and forget about their money problems.

Each item in the above list includes two statements, and the second statement does not necessarily follow from the first. More evidence is needed to make any possible connection.

ATTACKING THE PERSON

This fallacy flourishes at election time. Consider the example of a candidate who claims that her opponent failed to attend church regularly during the campaign. Candidates who indulge in personal attacks about private matters are attempting an intellectual sleight of hand. They want to divert our attention from the truly relevant issues.

APPEALING TO AUTHORITY

A professional athlete endorses a brand of breakfast cereal. A famous musician features a soft drink company's product in a music video. The promotional brochure for an advertising agency lists all of the large companies that have used its services.

In each case, the people involved are trying to win your confidence—and your dollars—by citing authorities. The underlying assumption is usually this: *Famous people and organizations buy our product. Therefore, you should buy it too.* Or: *You should accept this idea merely because someone who's well-known says it's true.*

Appealing to authority is usually a substitute for producing real evidence. It invites sloppy thinking. When our only evidence for a viewpoint is an appeal to authority, it's time to think more thoroughly.

POINTING TO A FALSE CAUSE

The fact that one event follows another does not necessarily mean that the two events have a cause-and-effect relationship. All we can actually say is that the events might be correlated. For example, as children's vocabularies improve, they can get more cavities. This does not mean that cavities

are the result of an improved vocabulary. Instead, the increase in cavities is due to other factors, such as physical maturation and changes in diet or personal care.

THINKING IN ALL-OR-NOTHING TERMS

Consider these statements: *Doctors are greedy. You can't trust politicians. Students these days are in school just to get high-paying jobs; they lack idealism. Homeless people don't want to work.*

These opinions imply the word *all.* They gloss over individual differences, claiming that all members of a group are exactly alike. They also ignore key facts—for instance, that some doctors volunteer their time at free medical clinics and that many homeless people are children who are too young to work. All-or-nothing thinking is one of the most common errors in logic.

BEGGING THE QUESTION

Speakers and writers beg the question when their colorful language glosses over an idea that is unclear or unproven. Consider this statement: *Support the American tradition of individual liberty and oppose mandatory seat belt laws!* Anyone who makes such a statement "begs" (fails to answer) a key question: Are laws that require drivers to use seat belts actually a violation of individual liberty? ✳

do you have a MINUTE?

Consider this statement: *Jay-Z sells more albums than Common, so Jay-Z must be a better musician.* Do you think that this statement is an example of a logical fallacy mentioned in this article? If so, which one?

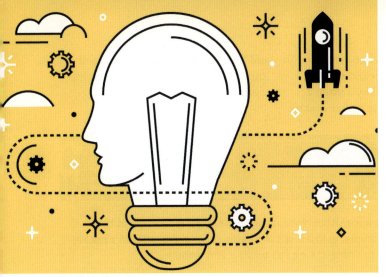

Vector Goddess/Shutterstock.com

Ways to create
IDEAS

Anyone can think creatively. Use the following techniques to generate ideas about anything—from solutions to math problems to plans for remodeling a house.

FOCUS AND LET GO

Focusing and letting go are alternating parts of the same process. First, focus on a problem or question for a short period of time. This uses the resources of your conscious mind. Then take a break and completely let go of finding a solution or answer. This gives your subconscious mind time to work. When you alternate focusing and relaxing, the conscious and subconscious parts of your brain work in harmony.

CULTIVATE CREATIVE SERENDIPITY

The word *serendipity* was coined by the English author Horace Walpole from the title of an ancient Persian fairy tale, "The Three Princes of Serendip." The princes had a knack for making lucky discoveries. Serendipity is that knack, and it involves more than luck. It is the ability to see something valuable that you weren't looking for.

History is full of people who make serendipitous discoveries. Country doctor Edward Jenner noticed "by accident" that milkmaids seldom got smallpox. The result was his discovery that mild cases of cowpox immunized them. Penicillin was also discovered by accident. Scottish scientist Alexander Fleming was growing bacteria in a laboratory petri dish. A spore of *Penicillium notatum,* a kind of mold, blew in the window and landed in the dish, killing the bacteria. Fleming isolated the active ingredient, which saved thousands of lives.

You can train yourself in the art of serendipity. Multiply your contacts with the world. Resolve to meet new people. Join a study or discussion group. Read. Go to plays, concerts, art shows, lectures, and movies. Watch television programs you normally wouldn't watch.

Keep your eyes open. You might find a solution to an accounting problem in a popular film. You might discover a topic for your next paper at the corner convenience store.

KEEP IDEA FILES

We all have ideas. People who treat their ideas with care are often labeled "creative." They are the people who recognize ideas *and* keep track of them.

One way to keep track of ideas is to write them down on 3×5 cards. You can also use digital tools to capture ideas. For example, create a word-processing document on a computer to record ideas as they occur to you.

In addition, keep a journal. Record observations about the world around you, conversations with friends, important or offbeat ideas—anything.

READ

To fuel your creativity, read voraciously. Consume books. Clip articles from printed magazines and newspapers. Keep up with your favorite blogs and websites, and bookmark pages to read in detail. Capture the most important ideas from all those sources, and add them to your journal.

PLAY WITH IDEAS

Once you gather ideas, look at them from several angles. Switch your attention from one aspect of an issue to another. Examine each fact you collect, and avoid getting stuck on one particular part of a problem. Turn a problem upside down by picking a solution first and then working backward. Ask other people to look at the data. Solicit opinions.

Also look for the obvious solutions or the self-evident "truths" about the problem—then toss them out. Ask yourself, "Well, I know X is true, but if X were *not* true, what would happen?" Or ask the reverse: "If that *were* true, what would follow next?"

Put unrelated facts next to each other, and invent a relationship between them, even if it seems absurd at first. Make imaginary pictures with the data. Condense it. Categorize it. Put it in chronological order. Put it in alphabetical order. Put it in random order. Order it from most to least complex. Reverse all of those orders. Look for opposites.

It has been said that there are no new ideas—only new ways to combine old ideas. Creativity is the ability to discover those combinations.

REFINE IDEAS AND FOLLOW THROUGH

Many of us ignore the part of the creative process that involves refining ideas and following through. How many great moneymaking schemes have we had that we never pursued? How many good ideas have we had for short stories that we never wrote? How many times have we said to ourselves, "You know, what they ought to do is attach two handles to one of those things, paint it orange, and sell it to police departments. They'd make a fortune." And we never realize that we are "they." Genius resides in the follow through—the application of perspiration to inspiration. ✖

Strategies for
EFFECTIVE
writing

Effective writing is essential to your success. While you're in school, you'll write papers, essay tests, and emails. In the work world, you can find yourself writing résumés, cover letters, proposals, reports, and presentations. All of these call on your ability to communicate ideas with force and clarity. Use the following strategies.

Schedule and list writing tasks. Divide the ultimate goal—such as a finished paper—into smaller steps that you can tackle right away. Estimate how long it will take to complete each step. Start with the date your final product is due and work backward to the present.

Say that the due date is December 1, and you have about 3 months to write the paper. Plan to get a first draft done by October 1 and a second draft done by November 1. That gives you time for big revisions and last-minute corrections.

One general guideline is to allow 50 percent of your project time for planning, researching, and writing the first draft. Then devote the remaining 50 percent to revising.

Jacob Lund/Shutterstock.com

Choose a topic. The most common pitfall is selecting a vague topic. "Harriet Tubman" is not a useful topic for your American history paper because it's too broad. Writing about her could take hundreds of pages. Instead, consider "Harriet Tubman's activities as a Union spy during the Civil War." This topic statement is more specific. It can also function as a working title for your paper.

Write a thesis statement. Clarify what you want to say by summarizing it in one concise and complete sentence. For example: "Harriet Tubman's activities with the Underground Railroad led to a relationship with the Union army during the Civil War." This sentence, called a *thesis statement*, refines your working title. It also helps in making a preliminary outline.

A thesis statement that's clear and to the point can make your paper easier to write. Remember, you can always rewrite your thesis statement as you learn more about your topic.

Consider your purpose. If you want someone to *think* differently, then make your writing clear and logical. Support your assertions with evidence.

If you want someone to *feel* differently, consider crafting a story. Write about a character your audience can empathize with, and tell how that character resolves a problem that the audience can relate to.

And if your purpose is to move the reader into *action*, explain exactly what steps to take. Also offer solid benefits for doing so.

Do initial research. At this stage, the objective of your research is not to uncover specific facts about your topic. That comes later. For now, you want to gain an overview of the subject. Discover the structure of your topic—its major divisions and branches.

Outline. To start an outline, gather a stack of 3 × 5 cards. Brainstorm ideas you want to include in your paper. Write one idea (word, phrase, or sentence) per card. Then experiment with the cards. Group them into separate stacks, each stack representing one major category. After that, arrange the stacks in a logical order. Finally, arrange the cards *within* each stack in a logical order. Rearrange them until you discover an organization that you like.

If you write on a computer or tablet, you can do the same thing. Just treat each of your ideas as a single paragraph. Arrange those paragraphs into related groups. Give each group a heading. For example, a paper about job hunting strategies might include headings such as *networking, resumés,* and *interviews*.

To simplify the process, don't create a complicated outline with many layers of ideas. Just arrange your headings in a logical order that moves the reader from your introduction to your conclusion.

Some people find that it works well to forget the words *outlining* and *writing* at this stage. Instead, they ease into the task with activities to generate ideas. You can free associate, cluster, meditate, daydream, doodle, draw diagrams, or talk into a voice recorder. Do anything that gets your ideas flowing.

Do in-depth research. Again, you can use 3 × 5 cards. They work wonders when you conduct research. Just write down one fact, quotation, or idea per card. This makes it easy to organize your ideas. You can also take notes with word-processing or note-taking applications for your computer, tablet, or smartphone.

While taking notes, *be sure to include a source for any material that you quote, paraphrase,* or *summarize* from an article, book, website, or interview. This is essential to avoid plagiarism.

Create a first draft. If you've planned your writing project, created an outline, and completed your research, you've already done much of the hard work. Now you can relax into writing.

To create your first draft, just arrange your notes to follow your outline. Then create a new document in which you transform those notes into a draft. State the main ideas in your own words. If you include a direct quote from one of your sources, put those words within quotation marks. Then cite the source in an endnote or footnote. (Ask your instructor for guidelines.) Also cite a source for any material that you paraphrase or summarize.

At this stage, don't worry about the quality of your writing. You can do that later, when you revise. Your goal at this point is simply to finish a first draft. Many writers prefer to get this done quickly. Their advice is to start writing and *keep writing* until you've covered the material in your outline.

Plan to revise several times. Once you've finished a first draft, let it sit for at least 24 hours. Then start revising. Make a clean copy of each revision, and let each revised draft sit for at least another 24 hours.

Keep in mind the saying "Write in haste; revise at leisure." When you revise, slow down and take a microscope to your work.

Cut. The first and most important step in revising is to look for excess baggage. Approach your first draft as if it were a chunk of granite from which you will chisel the final product. In the end, much of your first draft will be lying on the floor. What is left will be the clean, clear, polished product.

Sometimes the cuts are painful. Sooner or later, every writer invents a phrase that is truly clever but makes no contribution to the purpose of the paper. Grit your teeth and let it go.

Note: For maximum efficiency, make the larger cuts first—sections, chapters, pages. Then go for the smaller cuts—paragraphs, sentences, phrases, words. Stay within the word limit that your instructor assigns.

Paste. In deleting both larger and smaller passages in your first draft, you've probably removed some of the original transitions and connecting ideas. Your next task is to rearrange what's left of your paper so that it flows logically. Look for consistency within paragraphs and for transitions from paragraph to paragraph and section to section.

If your draft doesn't hang together, reorder the ideas. Imagine yourself with scissors and glue, cutting the paper into scraps—one scrap for each major point or event. Then paste these scraps down in a new, more logical order.

Fix. Now it's time to look at individual words and phrases. Define any terms that the reader might not know, putting them in plain English whenever you can.

In general, rely on vivid nouns and active verbs. Using too many adjectives and adverbs weakens your message and adds unnecessary bulk to your writing.

Also scan your paper for any passages that are written in the language of texting or instant messaging. Rewrite those into full sentences.

Proofread. In a sense, any paper is a sales effort. If you hand in a paper that is wearing wrinkled jeans, its hair tangled and unwashed, and its shoes untied, your instructor is less likely to buy it. To avoid this situation, format your paper following accepted standards for margin widths, endnotes, title pages, and other details. Also ask your instructor about when and on how to cite the sources used in writing

your paper. Finally, look over your paper with an eye for spelling and grammar errors.

When you're through proofreading, take a minute to savor the result. You've just witnessed something of a miracle—the mind attaining clarity and resolution. That's the *aha!* in writing. ✖

Planning and delivering a
PRESENTATION

Some people tune out during a presentation. Just think about all the times you have listened to politicians. Remember all the wonderful daydreams you had during their speeches.

g-stockstudio/Shutterstock.com

Your audiences are like you. To keep them tuned in to your presentation, use the following suggestions. You'll develop skills that can help you succeed in any course and advance in your career.

Start from your passions. If your instructor allows you to choose the topic of the presentation, then choose one that you find interesting. Imagine that the first words in your presentation will be: *I'm here to talk to you because I feel passionately about. . . .* How would you complete this sentence. Turn your answer into your main topic.

Analyze your audience. Remember that audiences generally have one question in mind: *So what?* Or, *Why does this matter to me?* They want to know that your presentation relates to their desires.

To convince people that you have something worthwhile to say, write down the main point of your presentation. See whether you can complete this sentence: *I'm telling you this because. . . .*

Communicate your message in three parts. Presentations are usually organized into three main sections: the introduction, the main body, and the conclusion.

In your introduction, state your main point in a way that gets attention. Then give your audience a hint of what's coming next. For example: "More people have died from hunger in the past 5 years than have been killed in all of the wars, revolutions, and murders in the past 150 years. Yet there is enough food to go around. I'm honored to be here with you today and share a solution to this problem."

A simple way to develop the body of your presentation—especially an informal one—is to list three questions that audience members are likely to ask about your topic. Write a clear, one-sentence answer to each of those questions. These answers are your main points. Support each point with facts, quotations, and interesting stories.

For the conclusion, summarize your key points and draw your conclusion in

a way that no one will forget. A simple standby is this: "In conclusion, I want you to remember three points. . . ."

Create speaking notes. Some professional speakers recommend writing out your speech in full and then putting key words or main points on a few 3×5 cards. Number the cards, so if you drop them, you can quickly put them in order again. As you finish the information on each card, move it to the back of the pile. Write information clearly and in letters large enough to be seen from a distance.

Other speakers prefer to use standard outlined notes instead of cards. Another option is concept mapping. Even an hour-long speech can be mapped on one sheet of paper.

Create supporting visuals. Presentations often include visuals such as flip charts or slides created with presentation software. These materials can reinforce your main points.

Remember that effective visuals complement rather than replace your speaking. If you use too many visuals—or visuals that are too complex—your audience might focus on them and forget about you.

Practice your presentation. The key to successful public speaking is practice. Commit to practice sessions by writing them down on your calendar or in a planner. When you practice, do so in a loud voice, which helps your audience to hear you.

Keep practicing. Avoid sounding as if you were reading a script. When you know your material well, you can deliver it in a natural way. Practice your presentation until you could deliver it in your sleep. Then run through it a few more times.

Watch the time. Time yourself as you practice. Aim for a lean presentation—just enough to make your point and avoid making your audience restless. Leave your listeners wanting more. The goal is to be brief and then to be seated.

Overcome fear of public speaking. Michael Motley, a professor at the University of California-Davis, distinguishes between two orientations to speaking. People with a *performance orientation* believe that the speaker must captivate the audience by using formal techniques that differ from normal conversation.

In contrast, speakers with a *communication orientation* see public speaking simply as an extension of one-to-one conversation. The goal is not to perform, but to communicate your ideas to an audience in the same ways that you would explain them to a friend.[3] In other words, focus on the content of your presentation—not on yourself. ✂

DISCOVERY / INTENTION STATEMENT

journal entry **8**

Take the next step in finding your speaking voice

What do you want to improve about your presentation skills? Thinking about past speeches you have made can help you with future presentations you make in the classroom and in the workplace. Being honest about your current skills will open you up to new strategies that will help you succeed.

Think beyond this text, as well. Look to successful speakers in your community or in the public eye. In light of their strengths, consider the speaking skills that you'd like to gain.

Discovery Statement
Think back to the last time you were called upon to speak before a group. Write down what you remember about that situation. For example, describe the physical sensations you experienced before and during your presentation, the overall effectiveness of your presentation, and any feedback you received from the audience.

I discovered that . . .

Intention Statement
Based on what you wrote previously, what would you like to do differently the next time you speak? Describe the most important thing that you could do to become a more effective speaker.

I intend to . . .

Action Statement
Now, review this chapter for five suggestions that could help you make your intention a reality.

Finally, choose *one* strategy that you will definitely use for your next presentation.

I will . . .

SKILLS *snapshot*

Take a minute to reflect on your responses to the Thinking & Communicating section of the Discovery Wheel. Reflect on the progress you've made since you did that exercise, and clarify your intentions to develop further mastery. Complete the following sentences:

Discovery

My self-score on the Thinking & Communicating section of the Discovery Wheel was . .

When asked to evaluate different opinions on an issue or choose among potential solutions to a problem, the first thing I do is . . .

When I hear an accomplished public speaker, the skill that I would most like to acquire is . . .

The biggest obstacle I face right now in becoming an effective writer is . . .

Intention

Based on these discoveries, I now intend to develop my skill in. . .

Action

The very next action I will take to develop that skill is. . .

do you have a
MINUTE

Choose a 1-minute strategy listed in this chapter and describe how you could expand it to 15 or 30 minutes of focused activity. For example: instead of writing just one sentence for the first draft of a paper or presentation, you could write one paragraph. Put your expanded strategy in writing.

Rawpixel.com/Shutterstock.com

Creating Positive Relationships in a Diverse World

why

Your "people skills"—including listening deeply and speaking compassionately—are as important to your success as technical skills.

how

Think of a time when you experienced an emotionally charged conflict with another person. Then scan this chapter for suggestions that can help you communicate your feelings and thoughts more skillfully in such situations.

what if ...

I could consistently create the kind of relationships that I've always wanted?

what is included...

do you have a minute?

In just 60 seconds you can make a positive impact on your relationships. For example:

- List the names of three people who have positively influenced your life.
- Contact one of these people to express your gratitude via email, letter, phone call, or personal conversation.

Choose your conversations and your community

Conversations can exist in many forms. One form involves people talking out loud to each other. At other times, the conversation takes place inside our own heads, and we call it *thinking*. We are even having a conversation when we read a magazine or a book, watch television or a movie, or write a letter or a report. These observations have three implications that wind their way through every aspect of our lives.

One implication is that conversations exercise incredible power over what we think, feel, and do. They shape our attitudes, our decisions, our opinions, our emotions, and our actions. If you want clues as to what a person will be like tomorrow, listen to what she's talking about today.

Second, given that conversations are so powerful, it's amazing that few people act on this fact. Most of us swim in a constant sea of conversations, almost none of which we carefully and thoughtfully choose.

The real power of this process lies in a third discovery: We can choose our conversations. Certain conversations create real value for us. They give us fuel for reaching our goals. Other conversations distract us from what we want. They might even create lasting unhappiness and frustration.

Suppose that you meet with an instructor to ask about some guidelines for writing a term paper. She launches into a tirade about your writing skills and lack of preparation for higher education. This presents you with several options. One possibility is to talk about what a jerk the instructor is and give up on the idea of learning to write well. Another option is to refocus the conversation on what you can do to improve your writing skills, such as working with a writing tutor or taking a basic composition class. These two sets of conversations will have vastly different consequences for your success in school.

Another important fact about conversations is that the people you associate with influence them dramatically. If you want to change your attitudes about anything—prejudice, politics, religion, humor—choose your conversations by choosing your community. Spend time with people who speak about and live consistently with the attitudes you value. Use conversations to change habits. Use conversations to explore new ways of seeing the world and to create new options in your life.

When we choose our conversations, we discover a tool of unsurpassed power. This tool has the capacity to remake our thoughts—and thus our lives. It's as simple as choosing the next article you read or the next topic you discuss with a friend.

Start choosing your conversations today, and watch what happens. ✖

POWER TOOLS
for listening and speaking

Observe a person in a conversation who is not talking. Is he listening? Maybe. Maybe not. Perhaps he's preparing his response or just daydreaming. Effective listening calls for concentration and energy. And it's worth the effort. People love a good listener. The best sales-people, managers, coworkers, teachers, parents, friends, and lovers are good listeners.

Speaking is a challenge too. You have been talking with people for most of your life. Often you manage to get your messages across. There are times, though, when you don't. Often, these times are emotionally charged.

Listening and speaking are skills that we get to practice for a lifetime. The quality of our lives depends on them. Use the suggestions in this article to take your skills to a new level.

CHOOSING TO LISTEN

To listen well, begin from a clear intention. *Choose* to listen well. Once you've made this choice, you can use the following techniques to be even more effective at listening.

Be quiet. Silence is more than stay-ing quiet while someone is speaking. Allowing several seconds to pass before you begin to talk gives the speaker time to catch her breath and gather her thoughts. She might want to continue. Someone who talks nonstop might fear she will lose the floor if she pauses.

If the message being sent is com-plete, this short break gives you time to form your response and helps you avoid the biggest barrier to listening—listen-ing with your answer running. If you make up a response before the person is finished, you might miss the end of

the message, which is often the main point.

In some circumstances, pausing for several seconds might be inappropriate. Ignore this suggestion completely, as you would in an emergency where immediate action is usually necessary.

Maintain eye contact. Look at the other person while he speaks. Main-taining eye contact demonstrates your attentiveness and helps keep your mind from wandering. Your eyes also let you observe the speaker's body language and behavior. If you avoid eye contact, you can fail to see *and* fail to listen.

This idea is not an absolute. Main-taining eye contact is valued more in some cultures than others. Also, some people learn primarily by hearing; they can listen more effectively by turning off the visual input once in a while.

Display openness. You can display openness through your facial expression and body position. Uncross your arms and legs. Sit up straight. Face the other person, and remove any physical barri-ers between you, such as a pile of books.

Send acknowledgments. Let the speaker know periodically that you are still there. Words and nonverbal gestures of acknowledgment convey to the speaker that you are interested and that you are receiving his message. These words and gestures include "uh-huh," "okay," "yes," and head nods.

These acknowledgments do not imply your agreement. When people tell you what they don't like about you, your head nod doesn't mean that you agree. It just indicates that you are listening.

Release distractions. Even when your intention is to listen, you might find your mind wandering. Thoughts about what *you* want to say or some-thing you want to do later might claim your attention. There's a simple solution: Notice your wandering mind without judgment. Then bring your attention back to the act of listening.

You can also set up your immediate environment to release distractions. Turn off or silence your cell phone. Stash your laptop and other digital devices. Send the message that your sole intention in the moment is to listen.

Another option is to ask for a quick break so that you can make a written note about what's on your mind. Tell the speaker that you're writing so that you can clear your mind and return to full listening.

Suspend judgments. Listening and agreeing are two different activities. As listeners, our goal is to fully receive another person's message. This does not mean that we're obligated to agree with the message. Once you're confident that you accurately understand a speaker's point of view, you are free to agree or disagree with it. The key to effec-tive listening is understanding *before* evaluating.

Choose when to respond. When we listen to another person, we often interrupt with our own stories, opin-ions, suggestions, and comments. To avoid this kind of one-sided conversa-tion, delay your verbal responses. This does not mean that you remain totally silent while listening. It means that you wait for an *appropriate* moment to respond.

Feed back meaning. Sometimes you can help a speaker clarify her message by paraphrasing it. This does not mean parroting what she says. Instead, briefly summarize. Feed back what you see as the essence of the person's message: "Let me see whether I understood what you said . . ." or "What I'm hearing you say is . . . ." Often, the other person will say, "No, that's not what I meant. What I said was. . . ." There will be no doubt when you get it right.

Notice verbal *and* nonverbal messages. You might point out that the speaker's body language seems to convey the exact opposite of what her words do. For example: "I noticed you said you are excited, but you look bored." Keep in mind that the same nonverbal behavior can have various meanings across cultures. Someone who looks bored might simply be listening in a different way.

Listen for requests and intentions. An effective way to listen to complaints is to look for the request hidden in them. "This class is a waste of my time" can be heard as "Please tell me what I'll gain if I participate actively in class." "The instructor talks too fast" might be asking "What strategies can I use to take notes when the instructor covers material rapidly?" Viewing complaints as requests gives us more choices. Rather than responding with defensiveness, we can decide whether to grant the request.

Allow emotion. In the presence of full listening, some people will share things that they feel deeply about. They might shed a few tears, cry, shake, or sob. If you feel uncomfortable when this happens, see whether you can accept the discomfort for a little while longer. Emotional release can bring relief and trigger unexpected insights.

Ask for more. Full listening with unconditional acceptance is a rare gift.

Many people have never experienced it. They are used to being greeted with resistance, so they habitually stop short of saying what they truly think and feel. Help them shed this habit by routinely asking, "Is there anything more you want to say about that?" This question sends the speaker a message that you truly value what she has to say.

Be careful with questions and advice. Questions are directive. They can take conversations in a new direction, which may not be where the speaker wants to go. Ask questions only to clarify the speaker's message. Later, when it's your turn to speak, you can introduce any topic that you want.

Also be cautious about giving advice. Unsolicited advice can be taken as condescending or even insulting. Skilled listeners recognize that people are different, and they do not assume that they know what's best for someone else.

CHOOSING TO SPEAK

Begin with a sincere intention to reach common ground with your listener. Then experiment with the suggestions that follow.

Replace "you" messages with "I" messages. It can be difficult to disagree with someone without his becoming angry or your becoming upset. When conflict occurs, we often make statements about the other person, or "you" messages:

- "You are rude."
- "You make me mad."
- "You don't love me anymore."

This kind of communication results in defensiveness. The responses might be similar to these:

- "I am not rude."
- "I don't care."
- "No, *you* don't love *me*!"

"You" messages are hard to listen to. They label, judge, blame, and assume things that may or may not be true. They demand rebuttal. Even praise can sometimes be an ineffective "you" message. "You" messages don't work.

Consider limiting your statements to descriptions about yourself. Replace "you" messages with "I" messages:

- "You are rude" might become "I feel upset."
- "You make me mad" could be "I feel angry."
- "You don't love me anymore" could become "I'm afraid we're drifting apart."

Suppose a friend asks you to pick her up at the airport. You drive 20 miles and wait for the plane. No friend. You decide your friend missed her plane, so you wait three hours for the next flight. No friend. Perplexed and worried, you drive home. The next day, you see your friend downtown.

"What happened?" you ask.
"Oh, I caught an earlier flight."
"You are a rude person," you reply.

Look for and talk about the facts—the observable behavior. Everyone will agree that your friend asked you to pick her up, that she did take an earlier flight, and that you did not receive a call from her. But the idea that she is rude is not a fact—it's a judgment.

She might go on to say, "I called your home, and no one answered. My mom had a stroke and was rushed to Valley View. I caught the earliest flight I could get." Your judgment no longer fits.

When you saw your friend, you might have said, "I waited and waited at the airport. I was worried about you. I didn't get a call. I feel angry and hurt. I don't want to waste my time. Next time, you can call me when your flight arrives, and I'll be happy to pick you up."

"I" messages don't judge, blame, criticize, or insult. They don't invite the other person to counterattack with more of the same. "I" messages are also more accurate. They report our own thoughts and feelings.

At first, "I" messages might feel uncomfortable or seem forced. That's okay. Your skill with using this technique will improve with practice.

Remember that questions are not always questions. You've heard these "questions" before. A parent asks, "Don't you want to look nice?" Translation: "I wish you'd cut your hair, lose the blue jeans, and put on a tie." Or how about this question from a spouse: "Honey, wouldn't you love to go to an exciting hockey game tonight?" Translation: "I've already bought tickets."

We use questions that aren't questions to sneak our opinions and requests into conversations. "Doesn't it upset you?" means "It upsets me," and "Shouldn't we hang the picture over here?" means "I want to hang the picture over here."

Communication improves when we say, "I'm upset," and "Let's hang the picture over here."

Choose your nonverbal messages. How you say something can be more important than what you say. Your tone of voice and gestures add up to a silent message that you send. This message can support, modify, or contradict your words. Your posture, the way you dress, how often you shower, and even the poster hanging on your wall can negate your words before you say them.

Most nonverbal behavior is unconscious. We can learn to be aware of it and choose our nonverbal messages. The key is to be clear about our intention and purpose. When we know what we want to say and are committed to getting it across, our inflections, gestures, and words work together and send a unified message.

Notice barriers to sending messages. Sometimes fear stops us from sending messages. We are afraid of other people's reactions, sometimes justifiably. Being truthful doesn't mean being insensitive to the impact that our messages have on others. Tact is a virtue; letting fear prevent communication is not.

Assumptions can also be used as excuses for not sending messages. "He already knows this," we tell ourselves.

Predictions of failure can be barriers to sending too. "He won't listen," we assure ourselves. That statement might be inaccurate. Perhaps the other person senses that we're angry and listens in a guarded way. Or perhaps he is listening and sending nonverbal messages we don't understand.

Or we might predict, "He'll never do anything about it, even if I tell him."

Again, making assumptions can defeat your message before you send it.

If you have fear or some other concern about sending a message, be aware of it. Don't expect the concern to go away. Realize that you can communicate even with your concerns. You can choose to make them part of the message: "I am going to tell you how I feel, but I'm afraid that you will think it's stupid."

Talking to someone when you don't want to could be a matter of educational survival. Sometimes a short talk with an advisor, a teacher, a friend, or a family member can solve a problem that otherwise could hurt your education.

Take these ideas to work. In the workplace, you will regularly meet new coworkers, customers, and clients. One of the most practical communication skills you can develop is the ability to hold one-on-one conversations. The ability to put people at ease through "small talk" makes you valuable to an employer. This is a high-level skill that depends on the ability to listen closely and speak skillfully. Using "I" messages and the other suggestions in this article can help you thrive at work. ✈

do you have a **MINUTE**?

Think of one distracting habit—such as checking your email or smartphone—that prevents you from listening fully when someone speaks to you. Write an Intention Statement about how you will replace that habit with one that helps you listen more effectively.

THRIVING
in a diverse world

If you truly value diversity, then you can discover ways to create positive relationships with people from other cultures. Use the following suggestions, and invent more of your own.

Rawpixel.com/Shutterstock.com

Start with self-discovery. One step to developing diversity skills is to learn about yourself and understand the lenses through which you see the world. One way to do this is to intentionally switch lenses—that is, to consciously perceive familiar events in a new way.

For example, think of a situation in your life that involved an emotionally charged conflict among several people. Now mentally put yourself inside the skin of another person in that conflict. Ask yourself, "How would I view this situation if I were that person?"

You can also learn by asking, "What if I were a person of the opposite gender? Or if I were a member of a different racial or ethnic group? Or if I were older or younger?" Do this exercise consistently, and you'll discover that we live in a world of multiple realities. There are many different ways to interpret any event—and just as many ways to respond given our individual differences.

Reflect on experiences of privilege *and* prejudice. For example, someone might tell you that he's more likely to be promoted at work because he's white and male—*and* that he's been called "white trash" because he lives in a trailer park.

See whether you can recall incidents such as these from your own life. Think of times when you were favored because of your gender, race, or age—and times when you were excluded or ridiculed based on one of those same characteristics. In doing this, you'll discover ways to identify with a wider range of people.

Look for differences between individualist and collectivist cultures. Individualist cultures flourish in the United States, Canada, and Western Europe. If your family has deep roots in one of these areas, you were probably raised to value personal fulfillment and personal success. You received recognition or rewards when you stood out from your peers by earning the highest grades in your class, scoring the most points during a basketball season, or demonstrating another form of individual achievement.

In contrast, collectivist cultures value cooperation over competition. Group progress is more important than individual success. Credit for an achievement is widely shared. If you were raised in such a culture, you probably place a high value on your family and were taught to respect your elders. Collectivist cultures dominate in Asia, Africa, and Latin America.

In short, individualist cultures often emphasize "I." Collectivist cultures tend to emphasize "we." Forgetting about the differences between them can strain a friendship or wreck an international business deal.

If you were raised in an individualist culture:

- *Remember that someone from a collectivist culture may place a high value on "saving face."* This idea involves more than simply avoiding embarrassment. This person may *not* want to be singled out from other members of a group, even for a positive achievement. If you have a direct request for this person or want to share something that could be taken as a personal criticism, save it for a private conversation.
- *Respect titles and last names.* Although Americans often like to use first names immediately after meeting someone, in some cultures this practice is acceptable only among family members. Especially in work settings, use last names and job titles during your first meetings. Allow time for informal relationships to develop.
- *Put messages in context.* For members of collectivist cultures, words

convey only part of an intended message. Notice gestures and other nonverbal communication as well.

If you were raised in a collectivist culture, you can creatively "reverse" the previous list. For example, keep in mind that direct questions from an American student or coworker are meant not to offend, but only to clarify an idea. Don't be surprised if you are called by a nickname, if no one asks about your family, or if you are rewarded for a personal achievement. In social situations, remember that indirect cues might not get another person's attention. Practice asking clearly and directly for what you want.

Look for common ground. Students in higher education often find that they worry about many of the same things—including tuition bills, the quality of dormitory food, and the shortage of on-campus parking spaces. More important, our fundamental goals as human beings—such as health, physical safety, and economic security—cross culture lines.

Look for individuals, not group representatives. Sometimes the way we speak glosses over differences among individuals and reinforces stereotypes. For example, a student worried about her grade in math expresses concern over "all those Asian students who are skewing the class curve." Or a white music major assumes that her black classmate knows a lot about jazz or hip-hop music. We can avoid such errors by seeing people as individuals—not spokespersons for an entire group.

Be willing to accept feedback. Members of another culture might let you know that some of your words or actions had a meaning other than what you intended. For example, perhaps a comment that seems harmless to you

is offensive to them. And they may tell you directly about it.

Avoid responding to such feedback with comments such as "Don't get me wrong," "You're taking this way too seriously," or "You're too sensitive." Instead, listen without resistance. Open yourself to what others have to say. Remember to distinguish between the *intention* of your behavior and its actual *impact* on other people. Then take the feedback you receive, and ask yourself how you can use it to communicate more effectively in the future.

Speak up against discrimination. You might find yourself in the presence of someone who tells a racist joke, makes a homophobic comment, or utters an ethnic slur. When this happens, you have a right to state what you observe, share what you think, and communicate how you feel. Depending on the circumstance, you might say:

- "That's a stereotype, and we don't have to fall for it."
- "Other people are going to take offense at that. Let's tell jokes that don't put people down."
- "I realize that you don't mean to offend anybody, but I feel hurt and angry by what you just said."
- "I know that an African American person told you that story, but I still think it's racist and creates an atmosphere that I don't want to be in."

Change the institution. None of us lives in isolation. We all live in systems, and these systems do not always tolerate diversity. As a student, you might see people of color ignored in class. You might see people of a certain ethnic group passed over in job hiring or underrepresented in school organizations. And you might see gay and lesbian students ridiculed or even threatened with violence. One way

to stop these actions is to point them out. Also talk to your academic advisor about the civil rights laws that apply to students at your school and how those laws are enforced.

Prevent cyberbullying. *Cyberbullying* means using digital technology to harass, humiliate, or intimidate. It can take many forms, such as these:

- An email or text message with a hostile or threatening tone
- Rumors about you that are posted on your Facebook page or other social networking profile
- Getting deleted from a "friend list" as a deliberate attempt to upset you
- An online profile that's created by someone who pretends to be you
- Any of the above that happens on a repeated basis.

Don't put up with cyberbullying in any form. Start by ignoring the harassment or getting offline for a while. If that's not enough, block the perpetrators by changing the privacy settings on your email and text-messaging software. You can also change the username, password, and email address used for your profiles on social networking websites.

If you discover a fake online profile about you, then contact the company that runs the website, and tell them to take it down. To find out how, go to the home page and look for a Help link. Click it and then look for a search box. Key in *safety tips, abuse,* or similar keywords.

Also keep an eye on your stress level. If cyberbullying makes it hard for you to carry out your daily activities, that's a definite sign to get professional help. Talk to your academic advisor and a counselor at the campus health service. This is a problem that can be solved. ✠

Practice the art of saying no

All your study plans can go down the drain when a friend says, "Time to parrr-ty!" Sometimes, succeeding in school means replying with a graceful no. Saying no helps you prevent an overloaded schedule that compromises your health, your relationships, and your grade point average.

Discovery Statement

We find it hard to say no when we make certain assumptions—when we assume that others will think we're rude or that we'll lose friends if we turn down a request.

But think about it: You are in charge of your time only when you have the option to say *no*. Without this option, you are at the mercy of anyone who interrupts you. These will not be relationships based on equality. People who care about you will respect your wishes.

Recall a situation when you wanted to say no to someone but did not. Were you making assumptions about how the other person would react? If so, describe what you were thinking.

I discovered that I . . .

Intention Statement

Next, consider some strategies for giving someone a *no* that's both polite and firm. For instance, you can wait for the request. People who worry about saying no often give in to a request before it's actually been made. Wait until you hear a question: "Would you go to a party with me?"

You can also remind yourself that one no leads to another yes. Saying no to a movie allows you to say yes to getting a paper outlined or a textbook chapter read. Then you can give an unqualified yes to the next social activity.

Describe any strategies that you plan to use the next time you find it difficult to say no.

I intend to . . .

Action Statement

You might find it easier to act on your intention when you don't have to grasp for words. Choose some key phrases in advance. For example: "That doesn't work for me today." "Thanks for asking; my schedule for today is full." Or, "I'll go along next time when my day is clear."

To effectively deliver my next *no*, I will say . . .

Managing
CONFLICT

Conflict management is one of the most practical skills you'll ever learn. Here are suggestions that can help. Think of ways to use them in a conflict that you face right now.

SET THE STAGE FOR A SOLUTION

Back up to common ground. Conflict heightens the differences between people. When this happens, it's easy to forget how much we still agree with each other.

As a first step in managing conflict, back up to common ground. List all of the points on which you are *not* in conflict. For example: "I know that we disagree about how much to spend on a new car, but we do agree that the old one needs to be replaced." Once you've got this perspective, you can build on it with the following strategies.

Commit to the relationship. The thorniest conflicts usually arise between people who genuinely care for each other. Begin by affirming your commitment to the other person: "I care about you, and I want this relationship to last. So I'm willing to do whatever it takes to resolve this problem." Also ask the other person for a similar commitment.

Allow strong feelings. Permitting conflict can also mean permitting emotion. Being upset is all right. Feeling angry is often appropriate. Crying is okay. Allowing other people to see the strength of our feelings can help resolve the conflict. This suggestion can be especially useful during times when differences are so extreme that reaching common ground seems impossible.

Expressing the full range of your feelings can transform the conflict. Often what's on the far side of anger

is love. When we express and release resentment, we might discover compassion in its place.

Notice your need to be "right." Some people approach conflict as a situation where only one person wins. That person has the "right" point of view. Everyone else loses.

When this happens, step back. See whether you can approach the situation in a neutral way. Define the conflict as a problem to be solved, not as a contest to be won. Explore the possibility that you might be mistaken. There might be more than one acceptable solution. The other person might simply have a different learning style than yours. Let go of being "right," and aim for being effective at resolving conflict instead.

Sometimes this means apologizing. Conflict can arise from our own errors. Others might move quickly to end the conflict when we acknowledge this fact and ask for forgiveness.

Slow down the communication. In times of great conflict, people often talk all at once. Words fly like speeding bullets, and no one listens. Chances for resolving the conflict take a nosedive.

When everyone is talking at once, choose either to listen or to talk—not both at the same time. Just send your message. Or just receive the other person's message. Usually, this technique slows down the pace and allows everyone to become more level-headed.

To slow down the communication even more, take a break. Depending on

the level of conflict, this might mean anything from a few minutes to a few days.

A related suggestion is to do something nonthreatening together. Share an activity that's not a source of conflict with the people involved.

Communicate in writing. What can be difficult to say to another person face-to-face might be effectively communicated in writing. When people in conflict write letters or emails to each other, they automatically apply many of the suggestions in this article. Writing is a way to slow down the communication and ensure that only one person at a time is sending a message.

There is a drawback to this tactic, though: It's possible for people to misunderstand what you say in a letter or email. To avoid further problems, make clear what you are *not* saying: "I am saying that I want to be alone for a few days. I am *not* saying that I want you to stay away forever." Saying what you are *not* saying is often useful in face-to-face communication as well.

Before you send your letter or email, put yourself in the shoes of the person who will receive it. Imagine how your comments could be misinterpreted. Then rewrite your note, correcting any wording that might be open to misinterpretation.

There's another way to get the problem off your chest, especially when strong, negative feelings are involved: Write the nastiest, meanest email response you can imagine, leaving off the address of the recipient so you don't accidentally send it. Let all of your frustration, anger, and venom flow onto the page. Be as mean and blaming as possible. When you have cooled off, see whether there is anything else you want to add.

Then destroy the letter or delete the email. Your writing has served its purpose. Chances are that you've calmed down and are ready to engage in skillful conflict management.

Get an objective viewpoint. With the agreement of everyone involved, set up a video camera, and record a conversation about the conflict. In the midst of a raging argument, when emotions run high, it's almost impossible to see ourselves objectively. Let the camera be your unbiased observer.

Another way to get an objective viewpoint is to use a mediator—an objective, unbiased third party. Even an untrained mediator—as long as it's someone who is not a party to the conflict—can do much to decrease tension. Mediators can help everyone get their point of view across. The mediator's role is not to give advice, but to keep the discussion on track and moving toward a solution.

Be willing to disagree. Sometimes we say all we have to say on an issue. We do all of the problem solving we can do. We get all points of view across. And the conflict still remains, staring us right in the face.

What's left is to recognize that honest disagreement is a fact of life. We can peacefully coexist with other people—and respect them—even though we don't agree on fundamental issues. Conflict can be accepted even when it is not resolved.

STATE THE PROBLEM

Now you can move into the actual content of the conflict. Using "I" messages, state the problem. Tell people what you observe, feel, think, and intend to do. Allow the other people in a particular conflict to do the same.

Each person might have a different perception of the problem. That's fine.

Let the conflict come into clear focus. It's hard to fix something unless people agree on what's broken.

Play with your problem statement. Remember that the way you state the problem largely determines the solution. Defining the problem in a new way can open up a world of possibilities. For example, "I need a new roommate" is a problem statement that dictates one solution. "We could use some agreements about who cleans the apartment" opens up more options, such as resolving a conflict about who will wash the dishes tonight.

Get all points of view out on the table. If you want to defuse tension or defensiveness, set aside your opinions for a moment. Take the time to understand the other points of view. Sum up those viewpoints in words that the other parties can accept. When people feel that they've been heard, they're often more willing to listen.

In times of conflict, we often say one thing and mean another. So before responding to what the other person says, use active listening. Check to see whether you have correctly received that person's message by saying, "What I'm hearing you say is . . . Did I get it correctly?"

FOCUS ON SOLUTIONS

Brainstorm. After stating the problem, dream up as many solutions as you can. Be outrageous. Don't hold back. Quantity—not quality—is the key. If you get stuck, restate the problem and continue brainstorming.

Choose. Next, review the solutions you brainstormed. Discard the

unacceptable ones. Talk about which solutions will work and how difficult they will be to implement. You might hit upon a totally new solution.

Implement. Choose one solution that is most acceptable to everyone involved, and implement it. Agree on who is going to do what by when. Then keep your agreements.

Evaluate. Finally, evaluate the effectiveness of your solution. If it works, pat yourselves on the back. If not, make changes or implement a new solution.

Remember to focus on the future. Instead of rehashing the past, talk about new possibilities. Think about what you can do to prevent problems in the future. State how you intend to change, and ask others for their contributions to the solution.

See the conflict within you. Sometimes the turmoil we see in the outside world has its source in our own inner world. A cofounder of Alcoholics Anonymous put it this way: "It is a spiritual axiom that every time we are disturbed, no matter what the cause, there is something awry with us."

When we're angry or upset, we can take a minute to look inside. Perhaps we are ready to take offense—waiting to pounce on something the other person said. Perhaps, without realizing it, we did something to create the conflict. Or maybe the other person is simply saying what we don't want to admit is true.

When these things happen, we can shine a light on our own thinking. A simple spot-check might help the conflict disappear—right before our eyes. ✺

do you have a
MINUTE?

Think of a person with whom you're currently in conflict. Write an Intention Statement describing how you will use a suggestion from this article the next time you speak to this person.

Developing
EMOTIONAL
intelligence

Vera Serg/Shutterstock.com

In his book *Working with Emotional Intelligence*, Daniel Goleman defines emotional intelligence as a cluster of traits:

- **Self-awareness**—recognizing your full range of emotions and knowing your strengths and limitations.
- **Self-regulation**—responding skillfully to strong emotions, practicing honesty and integrity, and staying open to new ideas.
- **Motivation**—persisting to achieve goals and meet standards of excellence.
- **Empathy**—sensing other people's emotions and taking an active interest in their concerns.
- **Skill in relationships**—listening fully, speaking persuasively, resolving conflict, and leading people through times of change.

Goleman concludes that "IQ washes out when it comes to predicting who among a talented pool of candidates *within* an intellectually demanding profession will become the strongest leader." At that point, emotional intelligence starts to become more important.[1]

If you're emotionally intelligent, you're probably described as someone with good "people skills." You're aware of your feelings. You act in thoughtful ways, show concern for others, resolve conflict, and make responsible decisions.

Your emotional intelligence skills will serve you in school and in the workplace, especially when you collaborate on project teams. You can deepen your skills with the following strategies.

RECOGNIZE THREE ELEMENTS OF EMOTION

Even the strongest emotion consists of just three elements: physical sensations, thoughts, and action. Usually they happen so fast that you can barely distinguish them. Separating them out is a first step toward emotional intelligence.

Imagine that you suddenly perceive a threat—such as a supervisor who's screaming at you. Immediately your heart starts beating in double-time, and your stomach muscles clench (physical sensations). Then thoughts race through your head: *This is a disaster. She hates me. And everyone's watching.* Finally, you take action, which could mean staring at her, yelling back, or running away.

NAME YOUR EMOTIONS

Naming your emotions is a first step to going beyond the "fight or flight" reaction to any emotion. Naming gives you power. The second that you attach a word to an emotion, you start to gain perspective. People with emotional intelligence have a rich vocabulary to describe a wide range of emotions. For examples, do an Internet search with the key words *feeling list*. Read through the lists you find for examples of ways that you can name your feelings in the future.

ACCEPT YOUR EMOTIONS

Another step toward emotional intelligence is accepting your emotions—*all* of them. This can be challenging if you've been taught that some emotions are "good," whereas others are "bad." Experiment with another viewpoint: You do not choose your emotional reactions. However, you can choose what you *do* in response to any emotion.

EXPRESS YOUR EMOTIONS

One possible response to any emotion is expressing it. The key is to speak without blaming others. Use "I" messages to state what you observe, what you feel, and what you intend to do.

RESPOND RATHER THAN REACT

The heart of emotional intelligence is moving from mindless reaction to mindful action. See whether you can introduce an intentional gap between sensations and thoughts on the one hand and your next action on the other hand. To do this more often:

- *Run a "mood meter."* Check in with your moods several times each day. On a 3 × 5 card, note the time of day and your emotional state at that point. Rate your mood on a scale of 1 (relaxed and positive) to 10 (very angry, very sad, or very afraid).
- *Write Discovery Statements.* In your journal, write about situations in daily life that trigger strong emotions. Describe these events—and your usual responses to them—in detail.
- *Write Intention Statements.* After seeing patterns in your emotions, you can consciously choose to behave in new

ways. Instead of yelling back at the angry supervisor, for example, make it your intention to simply remain silent and breathe deeply until he finishes. Then say, "I'll wait to respond until we've both had a chance to cool down."

MAKE DECISIONS WITH EMOTIONAL INTELLIGENCE

When considering a possible choice, ask yourself, "How am I likely to feel if I do this?" You can use "gut feelings" to tell when an action might violate your values or hurt someone.

Think of emotions as energy. Anger, sadness, and fear send currents of sensation through your whole body. Ask yourself how you can channel that energy into constructive action. ✖

Creating high-performance TEAMS

Your experience in higher education will include group projects. These projects can be fun and rewarding. They can also fall flat and lead to frustration. To avoid the pitfalls that take teams down, develop some specific skills in communication.

Konstantin Chagin/Shutterstock.com

MASTER YOUR FIRST MEETING

Following is a list of items to consider as you create the agenda for your first group meeting. For long and complex projects, you might need more than one meeting to get them done.

Introduce yourselves and share key information. Start with housekeeping details. Ask all group members to share their name and contact information—email address, phone number, and any other details that will help you stay in touch with each other.

Also share the times that you're available for group meetings. Make sure that someone captures all this information, puts it in writing, and distributes it to everyone in your group.

Define your outcome. Start your group project by describing your desired result in detail. Answer these questions: How will you know that your group has succeeded? What would a successful outcome look like and sound like? How would you feel when you produced it?

Brainstorm a list of answers, and ask someone in the group to record

them. Then combine the best words and phrases into a single sentence that expresses what you agree to produce. Check this sentence against the requirements of your assignment, and get feedback from your instructor or supervisor.

Choose roles. Groups do their best work when the members agree on the roles that they'll play. For example, the group *leader* sends out the agenda for meetings, starts and ends meetings, monitors the group's overall progress, and keeps the instructor up to date on the group's activity. A *timer* watches the clock to ensure that the group stays on schedule and gets to each item on the agenda. A *recorder* takes notes during meetings and maintains copies of all group-related materials. Beyond these basic roles, add any others that seem useful.

Plan tasks and time lines. Once your outcome and roles are clearly defined, create a step-by-step plan to actually get the work done. Answer these questions: To produce our outcome, what's the very next action we need to take? What actions will follow that one? Who will take each action? By when? List your planned actions in order, along with a due date and person responsible for each one. When an action is completed, your group leader can check it off.

Choose when and how to meet. End your first session by scheduling meetings for the rest of your project. Also choose how to stay in contact between meetings. Options include email, text, phone, and websites such as Google Drive (drive.google.com) that allow groups of people to share documents.

DEAL WITH CHALLENGES

Groups take time to gel. Don't expect yours to function perfectly right away. If conflicts develop between group members, view them as opportunities to develop your communication skills. The following suggestions will help.

Nothing drains energy from a group more than meetings that crop up at the last minute and waste everyone's time. If you're leading the group, be sure to give plenty of notice before meetings, and write up an agenda for each one. Keep it to three items, tops. To focus everyone's thinking, state each agenda item as a question to answer. Instead of listing "project schedule," for example, write: "When is a realistic time for our next meeting?"

When scheduling meetings, also set clear starting and stopping times. Then stick to them.

End each meeting by updating your list of planned actions. Make sure that each action is assigned to a specific person, with a clear due date. You'll know that meetings are working when the energy level in the group stays high and when people have clear commitments to take planned action before the next meeting. ✕

do you have a **MINUTE**?

Write a one-sentence Discovery Statement about a frustration you experienced with a group project. Follow up with a one-sentence Intention Statement describing how you will use a suggestion from this article.

SKILLS
snapshot

Take a minute to reflect on your responses to the Relationships section of the Discovery Wheel. Reflect on the progress you've made, and clarify your intentions to develop further mastery. Complete the following sentences.

Discovery

My score on the Relationships section of the Discovery Wheel was . . .

The technique that has made the biggest difference in my skill at listening is . . .

When I'm effective at managing conflict, I remember to . . .

Intention

By the time I finish this course, I visualize giving myself a score of _____ on the Relationships section of the Discovery Wheel.

More specifically, my goal is to . . .

Action

To achieve the goal I just described, the most important thing I can do next is to . . .

do you have a
MINUTE?

Take 60 seconds to describe how you'll know that you've reached a new level of mastery with your "people skills."

mimagephotography/Shutterstock.com

Choosing Greater Health

© 2019 Cengage Learning, Inc. May not be scanned, copied or duplicated, or posted to a publicly accessible website, in whole or in part.

why

Succeeding in higher education calls for a baseline of physical and emotional well-being.

how

Recall a time when illness, stress, or a simple lack of energy prevented you from doing something that was important to you. Then scan this chapter for at least three suggestions that can help you prevent a similar incident in the future.

what if …

I could meet the demands of daily life with energy and optimism to spare?

what is included…

do you have a minute?

In just 60 seconds you can make a positive impact on your health. For example:

- During long study sessions, take a 1-minute break every 20 minutes to stand, stretch, and walk.
- Go to the refrigerator and find one unhealthy food to throw away.
- Get on a yoga mat and do one "sun salutation."

Surrender

Life can be magnificent and satisfying. It can also be devastating. Sometimes there is too much pain or confusion. Problems can be too big and too numerous. Life can bring us to our knees in a pitiful, helpless, and hopeless state. A broken relationship, a sudden diagnosis of cancer, a dependence on drugs, or a stress-filled job can leave us feeling overwhelmed—powerless.

In these troubling situations, the first thing we can do is to admit that we don't have the resources to handle the problem. No matter how hard we try and no matter what skills we bring to bear, some problems remain out of our control. When this is the case, we can tell the truth: "It's too big and too mean. I can't handle it." In that moment, we take a step toward greater health.

Desperately struggling to control a problem can easily result in the problem controlling us. Surrender is letting go of being the master in order to avoid becoming the slave.

Many traditions make note of this idea. Western religions speak of surrendering to God. Hindus say surrender to the Self. Members of Alcoholics Anonymous talk about turning their lives over to a Higher Power. Agnostics might suggest surrendering to their intellect, their intuition, or their conscience.

In any case, surrender means being receptive. Once we admit that we're at the end of our rope, we open ourselves up to help. We learn that we don't have to go it alone. We find out that other people have faced similar problems and survived. We give up our old habits of thinking and behaving as if we have to be in control of everything. We stop acting as general manager of the universe. We surrender. And that creates a space for something new in our lives.

Surrender is not "giving up." It is not a suggestion to quit and do nothing about your problems. Giving up is fatalistic and accomplishes nothing. You have many skills and resources. Use them. You can apply all of your energy to handling a situation and still surrender at the same time. You can surrender to weight gain even as you step up your exercise program. You can surrender to a toothache even as you go to the dentist. You can surrender to the past while adopting new habits for a healthy future.

Surrender includes doing whatever you can in a positive, trusting spirit. Let go, keep going, and know when a source of help lies beyond you.

Hamamariah/Shutterstock.com

Olena Pivnenko/Shutterstock.com

Wake up to
HEALTH

Some people see health as just a matter of common sense. These people might see little value in reading a health chapter. After all, they already know how to take care of themselves.

Yet *knowing* and *doing* are two different things. Health information does not always translate into healthy habits.

We expect to experience health challenges as we age. Even youth, though, is no guarantee of good health. Over the last three decades, obesity among young adults has tripled. Twenty-nine percent of young men smoke. And 70 percent of deaths among adults ages 18 to 29 result from unintentional injuries, accidents, homicide, and suicide.[1]

As a student, your success in school is directly tied to your health. Stress and lack of sleep have been associated with lower grade point averages among undergraduate students. So have anxiety, depression, alcohol abuse,

tobacco use, and gambling.[2] Any health habit that undermines your success in school can also undermine your success later in life.

On the other hand, we can adopt habits that sustain our well-being. According to the Centers for Disease Control and Prevention, Americans could prevent 200,000 deaths each year by adopting the "ABCs of heart health"—aspirin when appropriate, blood pressure control, cholesterol management, and smoking cessation.[3]

Health also hinges on a habit of exercising some tissue that lies between your ears—the organ called your brain. One path to greater health starts not with new food or a new form of exercise, but with new ideas.

Consider the power of beliefs. Some of them create barriers to higher levels of health: "Your health is programmed by your heredity." "People can live until 90 even if they smoke and drink heavily." "Healthy food doesn't taste very good." "Over the long run, people just

don't change their habits." Be willing to test these ideas and change them when it serves you.

People often have vague beliefs about what the word *health* means. Actually, this word is similar in origin to *whole, hale, hardy,* and even *holy.* Implied in these words are qualities that most of us associate with healthy people: alertness, vitality, vigor. Healthy people meet the demands of daily life with energy to spare. Illness or stress might slow them down for a while, but then they bounce back. They know how to relax, create loving relationships, and find satisfaction in their work.

To begin a useful inquiry into health—and to open up new possibilities for your life—act on the idea that the main influence on your health is *you.* To flourish physically and mentally, look first to the ordinary decisions that you make every day. Reflect on what you choose to eat, how much you exercise, and how regularly you sleep.

Protect yourself from sexually transmitted infection

Make careful choices about sex. Abstain from sex, or have sex exclusively with one person who is free of infection and has no other sex partners. These are the most effective ways to prevent sexually transmitted infection (STI).

Make careful choices about drug use. People are more likely to have unsafe sex when drunk or high. Also remember that sharing needles or other paraphernalia with drug users can spread STIs.

Talk to your partner. Before you have sex with someone, talk about the risk of STIs. If you are infected, tell your partner.

Talk to your doctor. See your family doctor or someone at the student health center about STIs. Some methods of contraception, such as using condoms, can also prevent STIs. Also ask about vaccinations for hepatitis B and HPV infection, symptoms of STIs, and how to get screened for STIs.

Choose to
EXERCISE

Exercise promotes weight control and reduces the symptoms of depression. It also helps prevent heart attack, diabetes, and several forms of cancer.[5] In addition, exercise refreshes your body and your mind. If you're stuck on a math problem or blocked on writing a paper, take an exercise break. Use the following simple ways to include more physical activity in your life.

Stay active throughout the day. Park a little farther from work or school. Walk some extra blocks. Take the stairs instead of the elevator. For an extra workout, climb two stairs at a time. An hour of daily activity is ideal, but do whatever you can.

Adapt to your campus environment. Look for exercise facilities on campus. Search for classes in aerobics, swimming, volleyball, basketball, golf, tennis, and other sports. Intramural sports are another option.

Do what you enjoy. Stay active over the long term with aerobic activities that you enjoy, such as martial arts, kickboxing, yoga, dancing, or rock climbing. Check your school catalog for classes. Find several activities that you enjoy, and rotate them throughout the year. Your main form of activity during winter might be ballroom dancing, riding an exercise bike, or skiing. In summer, you could switch to outdoor sports. Whenever possible, choose weight-bearing activities such as walking, running, or stair climbing.

Get active early. Work out first thing in the morning. Then it's done for the day. Make it part of your daily routine, just like brushing your teeth.

Exercise with other people. Making exercise a social affair can add a fun factor and raise your level of commitment.

Before beginning any vigorous exercise program, consult a health care professional. This is critical if you are overweight, over age 60, in poor condition, a heavy smoker, or if you have a history of health problems.

do you have a MINUTE?

Incorporating exercise into your daily routine is easier than it might seem! The next time you are standing at the sink while you brush your teeth, try doing calf raises or marching in place.

The power of small daily choices

If you want to succeed at changing your health habits for the better, think small. That's a suggestion from Tom C. Rath, senior scientist at Gallup, Inc. and author of *Eat Move Sleep: How Small Choices Lead to Big Changes*.[6] He believes that every nutritious meal, every minute of exercise, and every good night's rest has an immediate and positive impact. Some of his suggested strategies are:

- Ask yourself whether the next food you put in your mouth is a net gain or a net loss. Repeat throughout the day.
- Gradually add sleep to your nightly schedule in 15-minute increments. Continue until you feel fully rested each morning.
- Put the healthiest foods in your home on a shelf at eye level or in a bowl on the counter.
- Identify one way you can work without sitting, right now. Test it out tomorrow.
- Pick one food or drink you sweeten regularly—artificially or without sugar—and consume it without the added sweetener for a week.
- Always leave the serving dishes in the kitchen; don't bring them to the table.
- Make every meal last at least 20 minutes.
- Engineer activity into your work. Have a standing or walking meeting. Get up and move every time you are on the phone.
- Use smaller cups, plates, and serving sizes to eat less.
- Go through the food in your house today. Get rid of a few unhealthy items that have been sitting on a shelf for months.
- Start every meal with the most healthy item on your plate, and end with the least.

Choose
EMOTIONAL HEALTH

A little tension before a test, a presentation, or a date is normal. That feeling can keep you alert and boost your energy. The problem comes when tension is persistent and extreme. That's when average levels of stress turn into *distress*.

You can take simple and immediate steps toward freedom from distress. Start with your overall health. Your thoughts and emotions can get scrambled if you go too long feeling hungry or tired. Eating well, exercising daily, and getting plenty of sleep are powerful ways to reduce stress. Also experiment with the following ideas for more emotional freedom.

Make contact with the present moment. If you feel anxious, see whether you can focus your attention on a specific sight, sound, or other sensation that's happening in the present moment. Focus all of your attention on one point—anything other than the flow of thoughts through your head. This is one way to use the "Power Process: Be here now" as a simple and quick stress-buster.

Scan your body. Simple awareness is an effective response to unpleasant physical sensations. Discover this for yourself by sitting comfortably and closing your eyes. Focus your attention on the muscles in your feet, and notice whether they are relaxed. Tell the muscles in your feet that they can relax. Move up to your ankles, and repeat the procedure.

Next, go to your calves and thighs and buttocks, telling each group of muscles to relax. Do the same for your lower back, diaphragm, chest, upper arms, lower arms, fingers, upper back, shoulders, neck, jaw, face, and scalp.

Use guided imagery. This technique can work especially well after making contact with the present moment. For example, you might imagine yourself at a beach. Hear the surf rolling in and the seagulls calling to each other. Feel the sun on your face and the hot sand between your toes. Smell the sea breeze. Taste the salty mist from the surf. Use all of your senses to create a vivid imaginary trip.

Don't believe everything you think. Stress results not from events in our lives but from the way we *think* about those events. One thought that sets us up for misery is: *People should always behave in exactly the way I expect.* Another one is: *Events should always turn out exactly as I expect.*

A more reasonable option is to dispute such irrational beliefs and replace them with more rational ones: *I can control my own behavior, but not the behavior of others.* And: *Some events are beyond my control.* Changing our beliefs can reduce our stress significantly.

Another way to deal with stressful thoughts is to release them altogether. Simply notice your thoughts as they arise and pass. Instead of reacting to them, observe them. You might enter a state of relaxation that also yields life-changing insights.

Solve problems. Although you can't "fix" an unpleasant feeling in the same way that you can fix a machine, you can choose to change a situation associated with that feeling. There might be a problem that needs a solution. Use distress as your motivation to take action.

Stay active. A related strategy is to do something—*anything* that's constructive, even if it's not a solution to a specific problem. The basic principle is that you can separate emotions from actions. It is appropriate to feel miserable when you do. It's normal to cry and express your feelings. It is also possible to go to class, study, work, eat, and feel miserable at the same time. Unless you have a diagnosable problem with your emotional health, continue normal activities until the misery passes.

do you have a MINUTE?

Close your eyes, relax, and spend 60 seconds to do the body scan suggested in this article.

—————————————————————

DISCOVERY STATEMENT

Asking for help

Think back to a time in your life when you experienced so much stress that you felt overwhelmed and doubted your ability to cope. Did your response to this situation include asking someone for help? Describe what happened and what you did to take care of yourself.

I discovered that I responded to stress by . . .

Share what you're thinking and feeling. There are times when negative thoughts and emotions persist even when you take appropriate action. Tell a family member or friend about your feelings. This is a powerful way to gain perspective. The simple act of describing a problem can sometimes reveal a solution or give you a fresh perspective.

Ask for help. Student health centers are not just for treating colds, allergies, and flu symptoms. Counselors expect to help students deal with adjustment to campus, changes in mood, academic problems, and drug use disorders.

Remember a basic guideline about *when* to seek help: whenever problems with your thinking, moods, or behaviors consistently interfere with your ability to sleep, eat, go to class, work, or sustain relationships.

Your tuition helps pay for health services. It's smart to use them. ✴

Asking for
HELP

The world responds to people who ask. If you're not consistently getting what you want in life, then consider the power of asking for help.

"Ask and you shall receive" is a gem of wisdom from many spiritual traditions. Yet acting on this simple idea can be challenging.

Some people see asking for help as a sign of weakness. Actually, it's a sign of strength. Focus on the potential rewards. When you're willing to receive and others are willing to give, resources become available. Circumstances fall into place. Dreams that once seemed too big become goals that you can actually achieve. You benefit, and so do other people.

Remember that asking for help pays someone a compliment. It means that you value what people have to offer.

Many will be happy to respond. The key is asking with skill.

ASK WITH CLARITY
Before asking for help, think about your request. Take time to prepare, and consider putting it in writing before you ask in person.

The way you ask has a great influence on the answers you get. For example, "I need help with money" is a big statement. People might not know how to respond. Be more specific: "Do you know any sources of financial aid that I might have missed?" Or: "My expenses exceed my income by $200 each month. I don't want to work more hours while I'm in school. How can I fill the gap?"

ASK WITH SINCERITY

People can tell when a request comes straight from your heart. Although clarity is important, remember that you're asking for help—not making a speech. Keep it simple and direct. Just tell the truth about your current situation, what you want, and the gap between the two. It's okay to be less than perfect.

ASK WIDELY

Consider the variety of people who can offer help. They include parents, friends, classmates, coworkers, mentors, and sponsors. People such as counselors, advisors, and librarians are *paid* to help you.

Also be willing to ask for help with tough issues in any area of life—sex, health, money, career decisions, and

more. If you consistently ask for help only in one area, you limit your potential.

To get the most value from this suggestion, direct your request to an appropriate person. For example, you wouldn't ask your instructors for advice about sex. However, you can share any concern with a professional counselor.

ASK WITH AN OPEN MIND

When you ask for help, see whether you can truly open up. If an idea seems strange or unworkable, put your objections on hold for the moment. If you feel threatened or defensive, just notice the feeling. Then return to listening. Discomfort can be a sign that you're about to make a valuable discovery. If people only confirm what you already think and feel, you miss the chance to learn.

ASK WITH RESPONSIBILITY

If you want people to offer help, then avoid statements such as "You know that suggestion you gave me last time? Wow, that really bombed!"

When you act on an idea and it doesn't work, the reason may have nothing to do with the other person. Perhaps you misunderstood or forgot

a key point. Ask again for clarity. In any case, the choice about what to do—and the responsibility for the consequences—is still yours.

ASK WITH AN OPENING FOR MORE IDEAS

Approaching people with a specific, limited request can work wonders. So can asking in a way that takes the conversation to a new place. You can do this with creative questions: "Do you have any other ideas for me?" "Would it help if I approached this problem from a different angle?" "Could I be asking a better question?"

ASK AGAIN

People who make a living by selling things know the power of a repeated request. Some people habitually respond to a first request with no. They might not get to yes until the second or third request.

Some cultures place a value on competition, success, and "making it on your own." In this environment, asking for help is not always valued. Sometimes people say no because they're surprised or not sure how to respond. Give them more time and another chance to come around. ✖

Alcohol and other drugs:
THE TRUTH

The truth is that using alcohol, tobacco, caffeine, cocaine, marijuana, and other drugs can be fun. The payoffs might include relaxation, self-confidence, excitement, or the ability to pull an all-nighter.

In addition to the payoffs, there are costs. And sometimes these are much greater than the payoff.

Lectures about drug use and abuse can be pointless. We don't take care of our bodies because someone says we should. We might take care of ourselves when we see that the costs of using alcohol and other drugs *outweigh* the benefits.

It's your body. You get to choose.

Some people will choose to stop using a drug when the consequences get serious enough. Other people don't stop. They continue their self-defeating behaviors, no matter what the consequences. Their top priority in life is finding and using drugs. At that point, the problem is commonly called addiction. The technical term for addiction is *alcohol use disorder* or *substance use disorder*. Fortunately, help is available.

As you choose your relationship with alcohol and other drugs, consider the following suggestions.

Use responsibly. Show people that you can have a good time without drugs. If you do choose to drink, consume alcohol with food. Pace yourself. Take time between drinks.

Avoid promotions that encourage excess drinking. "Ladies Drink Free" nights are especially dangerous.

Women are affected more quickly by alcohol, making them targets for rape. Also stay out of games that encourage people to guzzle. And avoid people who make fun of you for choosing not to drink.

Pay attention. Whenever you use alcohol or another drug, do so with awareness. Then pay attention to the consequences. Act with deliberate decision rather than out of habit or under pressure from others.

Look at the costs. There is always a tradeoff to dependence. Drinking six beers might result in a temporary high, and you will probably remember that feeling. You might feel terrible the morning after consuming six beers, but some people find it easier to forget *that* pain. Stay aware of how dependence makes you feel.

Before going out to a restaurant or bar, set a limit for the number of drinks you will consume. If you consistently break this promise to yourself and experience negative consequences afterward, then you have a problem.

Admit problems. People with active addictions are a varied group—rich and poor, young and old, successful and unsuccessful. Often these people do have one thing in common: They are masters of denial. They deny that they are unhappy. They deny that they have hurt anyone. They are convinced that they can quit any time they want.

They sometimes become so good at hiding the problem from themselves that they die.

Take responsibility for recovery. Nobody plans to become addicted. If you have pneumonia, you seek treatment and recover without shame. Approach addiction in the same way. You can take responsibility for your recovery without blame or shame.

Get help. Two broad options exist. One is the growing self-help movement. The other is formal treatment. People who seek help often combine the two.

Many self-help groups are modeled after Alcoholics Anonymous (AA)— one of the oldest and most successful programs in this category. Groups based on AA principles exist for many other problems as well.

Some people feel uncomfortable with the AA approach. Other resources exist for them, including private therapy and group therapy. Also investigate organizations such as Women for Sobriety, the Secular Organizations for Sobriety, and Rational Recovery.

Use whatever works for you. ✄

Now that you've reflected on the ideas in this chapter and experimented with some new strategies, revisit your responses to the Health section of the Discovery Wheel exercise. Also think about ways to develop more mastery in this area of your life. Complete the following sentences:

Discovery

My score on the Health section of the Discovery Wheel was . . .

To monitor my current level of health, I look for specific changes in . . .

After reading and doing this chapter, my top three health concerns are . . .

Intention

In response to those health concerns, I intend to . . .

Action

At the end of this course, I would like my Health score on the Discovery Wheel to be . . .

The most important health habit for me to adopt right now is . . .

do you have a MINUTE?

Take 60 seconds to practice a small new habit for better health. For example, walk one block. Eat one piece of fruit. As soon as you get home from school, text a loving message to one friend or family member.

Instead of seeing a career as something that you discover, see it as something you choose. You don't find *the right career.* You create *it.*

hxdbzxy/Shutterstock.com

Choosing Your Major & Planning Your Career

why

Your courses come alive when you connect them with a focus for your education—and a direction for the rest of your life.

how

Visualize yourself at your commencement ceremony, walking up the front of the room and receiving a diploma for your degree. Also imagine what you'd like to be doing during the year after you graduate. Preview this chapter for strategies that you can use to turn these images into reality.

what if ...

I could create the career and life of my dreams—starting today?

what is included ...

do you have a minute?

In just 60 seconds you can take action to create your future. For example:

- Go online to your school's website and look for information about the career center.
- Make an appointment with your academic advisor to talk about the procedure for declaring a major.
- Brainstorm a list of ideas for a business that you could start now or after you graduate.

Now consider the kinds of jobs that draw on these skills.

For example, you could transfer your skill at writing papers to a possible career in journalism, technical writing, or advertising copywriting.

You could use your editing skills to work in the field of publishing as a magazine or book editor.

Interviewing and research skills could help you enter the field of market research. And the abilities to plan, manage time, and meet deadlines will help you succeed in all the jobs mentioned so far.

The basic idea is to take a cue from the word *transferable*. Many skills you use to succeed in one situation can *transfer* to success in another situation.

According to the *AMA 2010 Critical Skills Survey*, conducted by the American Management Association, employers are now looking for people with a specific set of transferable skills—the "four C's":

- **Creative thinking**—creating ideas for new products and services, presenting those ideas to others, and working with teams to refine and implement them
- **Critical thinking**—stating questions precisely, examining a variety of possible answers, testing for logic and evidence, and using the results to make effective decisions and solve problems
- **Communication**—creating and sharing meaning through speaking, listening, writing, and reading
- **Collaboration**—working effectively with diverse teams to set shared goals and to meet them.

The concept of transferable skills creates a powerful link between higher education and the work world. Skills are the core elements of any job. While taking any course, list the specific skills you are developing and how you can transfer them to the work world. By uncovering these hidden assets your list of qualifications will grow as if by magic. ✖

Four ways to choose
YOUR MAJOR

1. DISCOVER OPTIONS

Follow the fun. Perhaps you look forward to attending one of your classes and even like completing the assignments. This is one clue to a choice of major. Another is to see whether you can find lasting patterns in the subjects and extracurricular activities that you've enjoyed over the years. Look for a major that allows you to continue and expand on these experiences.

Consider your abilities. In choosing a major, ability counts as much as interest. In addition to considering what you enjoy, think about times and places when you excelled. List the courses that you aced, the work assignments that you mastered, and the hobbies that led to rewards or recognition. Let your choice of a major reflect a discovery of your passions *and* strengths.

Pertusinas/Shutterstock.com

Link to long-term goals. Your choice of a major can fall into place once you determine what you want in life. Before you choose a major, back up to a bigger picture. List your core values, such as contributing to society, achieving financial security and professional recognition, enjoying good health, or making time for fun. Also write down specific goals that you want to accomplish 5 years, 10 years, or even 50 years from today.

Gather information. Check your school's catalog or website for a list of available majors. Here is a gold mine of information. Take a quick glance, and highlight all the majors that interest you. Then talk to students who have declared them. Also read descriptions of courses required for these majors. Do you get excited about the chance to enroll in them? Pay attention to your "gut feelings."

Also chat with instructors who teach courses in specific majors. Ask for copies of their class syllabi. Go to the bookstore and browse the required texts. Based on all this information, write a list of prospective majors. Discuss them with an academic advisor and someone at your school's career-planning center.

Consider a complementary minor. You can add flexibility to your academic program by choosing a minor to complement or contrast with your major. An effective choice of a minor can expand your skills and career options.

Think critically about the link between your major and your career. You might be able to pursue a rewarding career by choosing among *several* different majors. After graduation, many people are employed in jobs with little relationship to their major. And you might choose a career in the future that is unrelated to any currently available major.

2. MAKE A TRIAL CHOICE

Pretend that you have to choose a major today. Based on the options for a major that you've already discovered, write down the first three ideas that come to mind. Consider that list for a few days, and then choose just one.

3. EVALUATE YOUR TRIAL CHOICE

When you've made a trial choice of major, take on the role of a scientist. Treat your choice as a hypothesis, and then design a series of experiments to evaluate and test it. For example:

- Schedule office meetings with instructors who teach courses in the major.
- Discuss your trial choice with an academic advisor or career counselor.
- Enroll in a course related to your possible major.
- Find a volunteer experience, internship, part-time job, or service-learning experience related to the major.
- Interview students who have declared the same major.
- Interview people who work in a field related to the major and "shadow" them—that is, spend time with those people during their workday.
- Think about whether you can complete your major given the amount of time and money that you plan to invest in higher education.
- Consider whether declaring this major would require a transfer to another program or even another school.

4. CHOOSE AGAIN

Keep your choice of a major in perspective. There is probably no single "correct" choice. Odds are that you'll change your major at least once—and that you'll change careers several times during your life.

As you sort through your options, help is always available from administrators, instructors, advisors, and peers. Look at choosing a major as the start of a continuing path that involves discovery, choice, and passionate action. ✶

Declare your major today

Pretend that you are required to choose a major today. Of course, your choice is not permanent. You can change it in the future. The purpose of this exercise is simply to get started a process that will lead to declaring an official major.

Step 1 Discover options

Look at your school's catalog or website for a list of majors. Make a photocopy of that list or print it out. Spend at least five minutes reading through all the majors that your school offers.

Step 2 Make a trial choice

Next, cross out all of the majors that you already know are not right for you. You will probably eliminate well over half the list. Scan the remaining majors. Next to the ones that definitely interest you, write "yes." Next to majors that you're willing to consider and are still unsure about, write "maybe."

Now, focus on your "yes" choices. See whether you can narrow them down to three majors. Then complete the following sentence:

I discovered that my top choices for a major are . . .

Finally, write an asterisk next to the major that interests you most right now. *This is your trial choice of major.*

Step 3 Evaluate your trial choice

Congratulations on making your choice! Now take a few minutes to reflect on it. Think about whether it aligns with your interests, skills, and current career plans.

Begin with some research. Find out everything that you can about the major you've chosen for now. Look for information in your school's course catalog and website. Talk to instructors who offer courses in this major, and ask for copies of the syllabus. Also talk to students who've taken those courses and alumni who had the same major. (Your school's career center can help you contact these people.)

In addition, test your choice by direct experience. For example, register for a course that's required to complete the major. See if you can find internships, work-study assignments, and study abroad programs related to your choice of major.

List specifically what you will do to research and test your trial choice of major.

I intend to . . .

Move into action by listing one intention that you will complete within the next 24 hours:

I will . . .

Note that the process of researching and evaluating might confirm your trial choice—or lead to an entirely new choice. No problem. The main point is that you're actively engaged in the process of creating your future and getting better informed about this key choice in your academic life.

Start creating your
CAREER

Many people approach career planning as if they were panning for gold, sifting through the dirt, clearing dust, and throwing out rocks. They hope to strike it rich and discover the perfect career. Other people believe that they'll wake up one morning, see the heavens part, and suddenly know what they're supposed to do. Many of them are still waiting for that magical day to dawn.

Instead of seeing a career as something that you discover, see it as something you choose. You don't *find* the right career. You *create* it.

There's a big difference between these two approaches. Thinking that there's only one "correct" choice for your career can lead to anxiety: *Did I choose the right one? What if I made a mistake?*

Viewing your career as your creation helps you relax. You don't have to worry about finding the "right" career. Choose a career today, knowing that you can choose again later.

You can get a lot of help by visiting your school's career-planning office. Also consider the following suggestions.

REMEMBER THAT YOU HAVE A WORLD OF CHOICES

Our society offers a limitless array of careers. You no longer have to confine yourself to a handful of traditional categories, such as business, education, government, or manufacturing. People are constantly creating new products and services to meet emerging demands.

In addition, people are constantly creating new goods and services to meet emerging needs. For instance, there are people who work as *ritual consultants*, helping people plan weddings, anniversaries, graduations, and other ceremonies. *Space planners* help individuals and organizations arrange furniture and equipment efficiently. *Auto brokers* visit dealers, shop around, and buy a car for you. *Professional organizers* will walk into your home or office and advise you on managing time and paperwork.

The global marketplace creates even more options for you. Through Internet connections and communication satellites that bounce phone calls across the planet, you can exchange messages with almost anyone, anywhere. Your customers or clients could be located in Colorado or Panama. Your skills in thinking globally and communicating with a diverse world could help you create a new product or service—and perhaps a career that does not even exist today.

RETHINK THE ROLE OF PASSION

One common piece of career advice is to "follow your passion." In other words, choose a career based on what you *love* to do. Then you're more likely to excel.

There are some problems with this advice. For one, many people don't have a clear passion to follow. Also, passion doesn't always come first. You might find that your enjoyment of a task grows *after* you begin to master the skills that it requires.

In a competitive job market, you can benefit by considering two factors beyond passion.

The first factor is your level of skill. For example, someone can enjoy playing the guitar and never do it well enough to make a living as a musician. It pays to get honest feedback on how well you've mastered the skills that you bring to your career. Having passion for your work is not the same as being able to pay your bills.

The second factor is market demand. If your passion is teaching philosophy, for instance, you might have to wait for years for a job opening. In addition to thinking about what you love to do, ask yourself: *What skills are rewarded in the work world? What can I do that solves a problem or otherwise creates clear value to employers, clients, or customers?* Once you've identified some skills that interest you, follow the suggestion of comedian Steve Martin to "become so good they can't ignore you."[2] When you excel at skills that are valued in the marketplace, you're more likely to thrive in your career.

In summary, keep looking for connections between your passion, your skills, and market demand. Also remember that there's probably more than one career that can give you a satisfying career. Research indicates that gaining mastery and making a contribution to the world are key factors in job satisfaction.[3]

THINK LIKE AN ENTREPRENEUR

An *entrepreneur* is someone who owns or manages a business. An entrepreneur's goal is to make a profit. This usually means taking a risk—creating a product or service to offer the public and working hard to make sure that it sells.

Maybe you don't see yourself as an entrepreneur. Perhaps you'd rather find a steady job with a regular paycheck and a benefit package. This is a traditional goal of career planning, but one you might find difficult to achieve in the current economy.

One solution is to *think* like an entrepreneur, even if you don't intend to be one. This means that you take charge of your job security rather than depending on an employer. Some ways to do this are:

- Master skills that are valued in the marketplace.
- Stay on top of new developments in the work world.
- Build a strong network of people who can help you find a new job.
- Manage your own benefits by saving money for emergencies, health care, and retirement.
- Brainstorm ideas for a product or service that you could sell.
- Test those ideas with a part-time job or project that you develop outside of your regular work hours.

TEST YOUR CAREER CHOICE—AND BE WILLING TO CHANGE

Once you have some possible career choices, translate them into workplace experience. For example:

- Contact people who are actually doing the job you're researching, and ask them a lot of questions about what it's like (an *informational interview*).

- Choose an internship in a field that interests you.
- Get a part-time or summer job in your career field.

If you find that you wish to continue such experiences, then you're probably making wise career choices. In addition, the people you meet are possible sources of recommendations, referrals, and employment in the future.

If you did *not* enjoy your experiences, celebrate what you learned about yourself. Now you're free to refine your initial career choice or go in a new direction. ⚔

Write an Intention Statement about the career that interests you most right now and what you will do in the next 24 hours to learn more about it.

Another option: Don't plan your career

When they hear the term *career plan*, some people envision a long document that lists goals with due dates and action steps. This is certainly one way to create a vision for your life's work.

Consider another approach: *Don't* plan your career—at least in the conventional way. In an economy that's constantly shedding jobs and adding new ones, you might benefit from an alternative approach.

Choose your direction rather than your destination. Instead of listing specific jobs that you'd like to have in the years to come, get in touch with your values. Determine what matters to you most about working. Ask yourself these questions:

- Do you want to work primarily with people? Ideas? Specific products or materials?
- Do you want to manage people or answer only to yourself and a handful of clients?
- What's the one thing that you do best—and enjoy doing—that creates value for people?

Put your answers in writing, and revise them at least once each year. The result can be a stable and flexible direction for your career, no matter what happens to the economy.

Take one new step in that direction. Determine the very next action you will take to move in your chosen direction. Create an intention that you can act on immediately. If you want to become self-employed, for instance, then contact one person who started a successful business, and ask for an information interview.

Reflect on what you learned—and choose your next step. Write Discovery Statements about the results of acting on your intention. What did you learn? In light of those lessons, what is the *next* step you'll take to move in your desired career direction?

The key is to take frequent action and reflect on the results. This process of determining your values and aligning your actions can teach you much about the work world—and open up opportunities that you might have never planned.

Developing a professional
WORK ETHIC

Through their behavior at school and at work, some people give the impression that they are merely warming chairs or taking up space. They perform just up to minimum requirements without much energy, enthusiasm, or commitment.

Another option is to demonstrate a *professional work ethic*. You'll see those three words in many job descriptions. They're not just filler. Employers value people who stand out from the crowd and demonstrate excellence.

START WITH THIS QUESTION

If you were employed as a student, would you be earning your wages? Consider that you *are*, in fact, employed as a student. You are paying a big price for the privilege of getting an education. Get the most value by spending as much time, attention, and energy on school as you would on a well-paying job.

FOCUS ON YOUR OWN PERFORMANCE

Your coworkers will be imperfect. Some might be irritating and incompetent. Good news: You don't have to fix them. In fact, you *can't* fix them. You can only control your own behavior. What other people do is up to them.

If other people waste your time with idle conversations, avoid the temptation to complain. Instead, say, "I'm swamped with work. Let's set a time to talk when I can give you my full attention." If someone schedules a meeting with no clear purpose, say, "Tell me more about why we're getting together and how I can contribute." Keep the conversation focused on solutions that you can implement.

DEMONSTRATE INITIATIVE

Demonstrating initiative means thinking carefully before making such statements as these:

- "I'm not going to do that—it's not in my job description."
- "I don't get paid enough to do that."
- "This problem has been around for years, and it's here to stay."
- "I'll wait until I get a promotion, then I'll think about getting involved."

Remember that you don't need a new job title in order to become a leader. When you spot a problem in your workplace, describe it in an objective way—without judgment or blame. Stick to the facts about what's working and what's not working. Then offer a possible solution. Better yet, offer several solutions.

DEMONSTRATE HUMILITY

During the course of your career, you'll meet people who value prestige above all else. These people tend to be fussy about their job title and position on the company's organization chart. They typically consider certain tasks to be "beneath" them. If they think that their achievements are ignored, they take offense and look for ways to get revenge.

In contrast, people with a professional work ethic see what needs to be done and pitch in. Instead of worrying about status or recognition, they join a team and look for ways to contribute.

Humility is a word that's often misunderstood. It does not mean downplaying your strengths or being the first to take blame. The true mark of a humble person is treating everyone in a workplace—from the janitor to the chief executive officer—with respect. Humility also means that you:

- **Respect your colleagues' workloads.** This attitude manifests in many behaviors. When you want to speak with someone, for example, first ask: "Is this a good time to talk?" Instead of running to coworkers every time that you get stuck, keep a running list of questions to ask each person. Send emails only when necessary, keeping them short and informative. And if you schedule a meeting, make sure to have a focused agenda and clear ending time.
- **Assume the posture of a learner.** A professional doesn't pretend to know all the answers. She asks other people for their suggestions. She respects points of view that differ from her own. And she refuses to criticize an idea until she's taken the time to fully understand it.
- **Admit mistakes.** A professional is open to coaching. He routinely asks for feedback, and he receives it without becoming defensive. If he makes an error, he quickly admits it. He also apologizes and looks for ways to make amends.
- **Give others credit.** When a project goes well, unprofessional people try to take credit. In contrast, professional people look for ways to *give* credit. They make a habit of expressing appreciation for the contributions of other people. ✄

Discover the
HIDDEN
job market

One of the most useful job skills you can ever develop is the ability to discover job openings *before* they are advertised. In fact, many openings exist even though they are never posted. This is the hidden job market.

Santiago Cornejo/Shutterstock.com

Conventional job hunting is passive. It relies on sending out résumés and waiting for responses. Instead, get active and tap the hidden job market. The following suggestions will get you started.

THINK LIKE AN EMPLOYER

Imagine yourself working as the hiring manager for a small business or head of human resources for a larger company. Your organization has a job opening, and your task is to fill it as soon as possible. You have the following options:

1. Hiring someone you know—a current or former employee or intern—with appropriate qualifications
2. Hiring someone who is *recommended* by a current or former employee or intern
3. Asking other members of your professional network to recommend a person for the job
4. Hiring someone else who has already contacted you and demonstrated that he or she has the appropriate qualifications
5. Contracting with an employment agency to screen potential applicants
6. Running blind ads in newspapers or posting openings online—and preparing for the dreaded onslaught of résumés.

If you're like most people in charge of hiring, you'll choose from options 1 through 4 whenever possible. That makes sense: You'd prefer to hire someone you know well or have met.

This is probably safer than risking your luck on a total stranger.

Unfortunately, many job hunters rely primarily on options 5 and 6. The traditional job-hunting method proceeds in *exactly the opposite direction* that employers use. No wonder people get frustrated.

To prevent this disconnection, think like an employer. Determine the specific job that you want and then get to know people. Do research to find organizations that interest you. Find out who does the hiring at those organizations, and contact those people directly.

DISCOVER YOUR NETWORK

You already have a network. The key is to discover it and develop it.

Begin by listing contacts—any person who can help you find a job. Contacts can include roommates, classmates, teachers, friends, relatives, and their friends. Also list former employers and current employers.

In addition, go to your school's alumni office and see if you can get contact information for past graduates—especially people who are working in your career field. This is a rich source of contacts that many students ignore.

Start your contact list now. List each person's name, phone number, and email address. Use word-processing, database, or contact-management software, or an app on your smartphone.

CONTACT PEOPLE IN YOUR NETWORK

Next, send a short email to a person on your list—someone who's doing the

kind of work that you'd love to do. Invite that person to coffee or lunch. If that's not feasible, then ask for a time to talk together on the phone. Explain that you'd like to have a 20-minute conversation to learn more about what the job entails. In other words, you're asking for an *information interview* rather than a job interview.

EXPAND YOUR NETWORK

Also tap the power of the Internet. Get the name of the person that you'd like to meet, and key it into your favorite search engine. Scan the search results to find out whether this person has a website, blog, or both. Also look for their presence on social networks such as Facebook, Twitter, and LinkedIn. With this information, you can do many things to connect. For example:

- Comment on a blog post that the person wrote.
- Join Twitter and post an update about this person or "retweet" one of their updates.
- Create your own website, add a blog, and write a post about this person.
- Send a short email—or handwritten note—that expresses your appreciation for the work the person does.

In any case, do not ask anything of people at this stage. Your goal is simply to show up on their personal "radar." Over time, they might initiate a contact with you. When this happens, celebrate. You're tapping the hidden job market. ✄

The Discovery Wheel reloaded

The purpose of this text is to give you the opportunity to adopt habits that promote success. This exercise gives you a chance to see what behaviors you have changed on your journey toward becoming a master student. Answer each question quickly and honestly. Record your results on the Discovery Wheel that follows, and then compare it with the one you completed in the Introduction to this text.

As you complete this self-evaluation, keep in mind that *your scores might be lower here than on your earlier Discovery Wheel.* That's okay. Lower scores might result from increased self-awareness, honesty, and other valuable assets.

As you did with the earlier Discovery Wheel, read the following statements and give yourself points for each one, using the point system described. Then add up your point total for each category and shade the Discovery Wheel to the appropriate level.

5 points	This statement is always or almost always true of me.
4 points	This statement is often true of me.
3 points	This statement is true of me about half the time.
2 points	This statement is seldom true of me.
1 point	This statement is never or almost never true of me.

1 Purpose

_____ I can clearly state my overall purpose in life.
_____ I can explain how school relates to what I plan to do after I graduate.
_____ I capture key insights in writing and clarify exactly how I intend to act on them.
_____ I am skilled at making transitions.
_____ I seek out and use resources to support my success.
_____ **Total Score: Purpose**

2 Learning Styles

_____ I enjoy learning.
_____ I make a habit of assessing my personal strengths and areas for improvement.
_____ I monitor my understanding of a topic and change learning strategies if I get confused.
_____ I use my knowledge of various learning styles to support my success in school.
_____ I am open to different points of view on almost any topic.
_____ **Total Score: Learning Styles**

3 Time & Money

_____ I can clearly describe what I want to experience in major areas of my life, including career, relationships, financial well-being, and health.
_____ I set goals and periodically review them.
_____ I plan each day and often accomplish what I plan.
_____ I will have enough money to complete my education.
_____ I monitor my income, keep track of my expenses, and live within my means.
_____ **Total Score: Time & Money**

4 Reading

_____ I ask myself questions about what I'm reading.
_____ I preview and review reading assignments.
_____ I relate what I read to my life.
_____ I select strategies to fit the type of material I'm reading.
_____ When I don't understand what I'm reading, I note my questions and find answers.
_____ **Total Score: Reading**

5 Notes

_____ When I am in class, I focus my attention.

_____ I take notes in class.

_____ I can explain various methods for taking notes, and I choose those that work best for me.

_____ I distinguish key points from supporting examples.

_____ I put important concepts into my own words.

_____ **Total Score: Notes**

6 Memory & Tests

_____ The way that I talk about my value as a person is independent of my grades.

_____ I often succeed at predicting test questions.

_____ I review for tests throughout the term.

_____ I manage my time during tests.

_____ I use techniques to remember key facts and ideas.

_____ **Total Score: Memory & Tests**

7 Information Literacy

_____ I choose appropriate topics for research projects.

_____ I translate topics into questions that effectively guide my research.

_____ I find credible sources of information to answer my questions.

_____ I think critically about information that I find.

_____ I translate the results of my research into effective speaking and writing.

_____ **Total Score: Information Literacy**

8 Thinking & Communicating

_____ I use brainstorming to generate solutions to problems.

_____ I can detect common errors in logic and gaps in evidence.

_____ When researching, I find relevant facts and properly credit their sources.

_____ I edit my writing for clarity, accuracy, and coherence.

_____ I prepare and deliver effective presentations.

_____ **Total Score: Thinking & Communicating**

9 Relationships

_____ Other people tell me that I am a good listener.

_____ I communicate my upsets without blaming others.

_____ I build rewarding relationships with people from other backgrounds.

_____ I effectively resolve conflict.

_____ I participate effectively in teams and take on leadership roles.

_____ **Total Score: Relationships**

10 Health

_____ I have enough energy to study, attend classes, and enjoy other areas of my life.

_____ The way I eat supports my long-term health.

_____ I exercise regularly.

_____ I can cope effectively with stress.

_____ I'm in control of alcohol or other drugs I put in my body.

_____ **Total Score: Health**

11 Major & Career

_____ I have a detailed list of my skills.

_____ I have a written career plan and update it regularly.

_____ I use the career-planning services at my school.

_____ I participate in internships, extracurricular activities, information interviews, and on-the-job experiences to test and refine my career plan.

_____ I have declared a major related to my interests, skills, and core values.

_____ **Total Score: Major & Career**

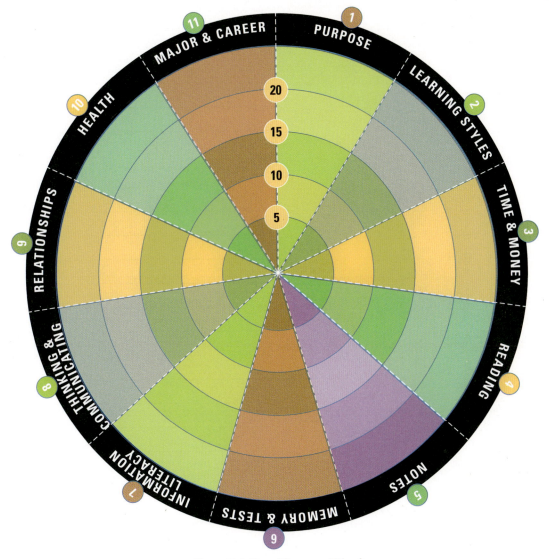

Figure 10.1 **Your Discovery Wheel**

Using the total score from each category, shade in each section of the blank Discovery Wheel. If you want, use different colors. For example, you could use green for areas you want to work on.

REFLECT ON YOUR DISCOVERY WHEEL

Take this opportunity to review both of the Discovery Wheels you completed in this text. Write your scores from each section of the Discovery Wheel from the Introduction in the chart below. Then add your scores for each section of the Discovery Wheel that you just completed.

	Introduction	Chapter 10
Purpose		
Learning Styles		
Time and Money		
Reading		
Notes		
Memory and Tests		
Technology		
Thinking and Communicating		
Relationships		
Health		
Major and Career		

Finally, summarize your insights from doing the Discovery Wheels. Then declare how you will use these insights to promote your continued success.

Comparing the Discovery Wheel in this chapter with the Discovery Wheel in the Introduction, I discovered that I . . .

_____

_____

_____

_____

_____

_____

_____

_____

_____

_____

_____

_____

_____

In the next six months, I intend to review the following articles from this text for additional suggestions I could use:

_____

_____

_____

_____

_____

_____

_____

_____

_____

_____

_____

_____

_____

_____

_____

_____

Now that you're done—
BEGIN

You are on the edge of a universe so miraculous and full of wonder that your imagination, even at its most creative moment, cannot encompass it. Paths are open to lead you to worlds beyond your wildest dreams.

If that sounds like a pitch for the latest recreational drug, it might be. This drug is adrenaline. It's automatically generated in your body when you are learning, taking risks, achieving goals, and discovering new worlds inside and outside your skin. This is a path of mastery that you can travel for the rest of your life.

Consider that you can create the life of your dreams. Your responses to any of the suggestions, exercises, and Journal Entries in this text can lead you to think new thoughts, say new things, and do what you never believed you could do. If you're willing to master new ways of learning, then the possibilities are endless. Any of the following suggestions can help.

Keep a journal. Continue writing Discovery Statements, writing Intention Statements, and taking action. The result will be continuous learning. Also keep a notebook full of your favorite quotations, lists of books to read, ideas for future projects, and any other ideas that you want to remember.

Take an unrelated class. Sign up for a class that is totally unrelated to your major. If you are studying economics, take a physics course. If you are planning to be a doctor, take an accounting course. Take a course that will help you develop new computer skills and expand your possibilities for online learning.

In addition to formal courses offered at your school, check into local community education courses. They offer a low-cost alternative that poses no threat to your grade point average.

Travel. See the world. Visit new neighborhoods. Travel to other countries. Explore. Find out what it looks like inside buildings that you normally have no reason to enter, museums that you never found interesting before, cities that are out of the way, and far-off places that require planning and saving to reach.

Get counseling. Solving emotional problems is not the only reason to visit a counselor, therapist, or psychologist. These people are excellent resources for personal growth. You can use counseling to look at and talk about yourself in ways that might be uncomfortable for anyone except a trained professional.

Form a support group. A well-organized study group can promote your success in school. An organized support group can help you reach goals in other areas of your life. Groups can brainstorm strategies for job hunting, career planning, parenting, relationships, spiritual growth, and reaching any goal you choose.

Find a mentor—and become one. Seek coaching from experienced people whom you respect and admire. Ask them to be sounding boards for your plans and ideas. Many people are flattered to be asked.

You can also become a mentor. If you want to perfect your skills as a master student, teach them to someone else. Offer to coach another student in study skills in exchange for child care, free lunches, or something else you value.

Consider further education and training. Your career plan might call for continuing education, additional certifications, or an advanced degree. Remember that the strategies in this text can help you gain new knowledge and skills at any point in your life.

Redo this text. If you didn't get everything you wanted from this text, it's not too late. You can read part of it—or all of it—again at any time.

As you redo this text or any part of it, reconsider techniques that you skimmed over or skipped before. They might work for you now. Modify the suggestions, or add new ones. Redoing this text can refresh and fine-tune your habits.

Another way to redo this text is to retake your student success course. People who do this often say that the second time is very different from the first. They pick up ideas and techniques that they missed the first time around and gain deeper insight into things they already know. ✖

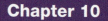
If you fully participated with this chapter, you've got a lot of answers to the opening question: What's next? Reflect on these answers in light of your responses to the Major & Career section of the Discovery Wheel.

Discovery

My score on the Major & Career section on the Discovery Wheel was . . .

What I want most as a result of completing the requirements for my major is to . . .

Three transferable skills that I've already developed are . . .

Three new transferable skills that I want to develop are . . .

What I want most from any career I choose is . . .

Intention

Based on these discoveries, I intend to major in . . .

I also intend to pursue a career in . . .

Action

The very next step that I will take to meet my career goal is . . .

do you have a
MINUTE?

Take one more opportunity to practice the time management skill of translating large goals into specific actions. List three 60-second tasks that will help you complete the actions you listed above:

Endnotes

INTRODUCTION

1. Charles Duhigg, *The Power of Habit: Why We Do What We Do in Life and Business* (New York: Random House, 2012), 276–286.

CHAPTER 1

1. David A. Kolb, *Experiential Learning: Experience as the Source of Learning and Development* (Englewood Cliffs, NJ: Prentice Hall, 1984).

CHAPTER 2

1. Jane B. Burka and Lenora M. Yuen, *Procrastination: Why You Do It, What to Do about It* (Boston, MA: Da Capo, 2004).

CHAPTER 3

1. Peter C. Brown, Henry L. Roediger III, and Mark A. McDaniel. Make It Stick: The Science of Successful Learning (Cambridge, MA: Harvard University Press, 2014).

CHAPTER 4

1. Gayle A. Brazeau, "Handouts in the Classroom: Is Note Taking a Lost Skill?" *American Journal of Pharmaceutical Education* 70, no. 2 (April 15, 2006): 38.

2. Walter Pauk and Ross J. Q. Owens, *How to Study in College*, 10th ed. (Boston: Cengage Learning, 2011).

3. Joseph Novak and D. Bob Gowin, *Learning How to Learn* (New York: Cambridge University Press, 1984).

CHAPTER 5

1. This article incorporates detailed suggestions from reviewer Frank Baker.

CHAPTER 6

1. Nicholas Carr, "Is Google Making Us Stupid?" *The Atlantic*, July 2008, accessed April 2, 2017 from http://www.theatlantic.com /magazine/archive/2008/07/is-google-making-us-stupid/6868/.

2. The terms waiting for list and someday/maybe list are taken from David Allen, *Getting Things Done: The Art of Stress-Free Productivity* (New York: Penguin, 2015).

CHAPTER 7

1. L. W. Anderson and D. R. Krathwohl, *A Taxonomy for Learning, Teaching, and Assessing: A Revision of Bloom's Taxonomy of Educational Objectives* (New York: Addison Wesley Longman, 2001).

2. Quoted in Arthur L. Costa and Bena Kallick, "Describing 16 Habits of Mind," accessed April 2, 2017 from https://thinkerstoolbox. wikispaces.com/file/view/Description.pdf/211201798/Description .pdf.

3. M. T. Motley, *Overcoming Your Fear of Public Speaking: A Proven Method* (New York: Houghton Mifflin, 1998).

CHAPTER 8

1. Daniel Goleman, *Emotional Intelligence: Why It Can Matter More Than IQ* (New York: Bantam, 1995), xiv–xv.

CHAPTER 9

1. Centers for Disease Control and Prevention, "Health Habits of Adults Aged 18–29 Highlighted in Report on Nation's Health," February 18, 2009, accessed April 2, 2017 from www.cdc.gov /media/pressrel/2009/r090218.htm.

2. American College Health Association, "National College Health Assessment: Undergraduate Students," Fall 2015, accessed April 2, 2017 from http://www.achancha.org/docs/NCHA -II_FALL_2015_UNDERGRADUATE_REFERENCE_GROUP _EXECUTIVE_SUMMARY.pdf.

3. Centers for Disease Control, "CDC Finds 200,000 Heart Disease and Stroke Deaths Could Be Prevented," September 3, 2013, accessed April 2, 2017 from http://www.cdc.gov/media /releases/2013/p0903-vs-heart-disease.html.

4. U. S. Department of Agriculture and Health and Human Services, "2015-2020 Dietary Guidelines for Americans," accessed April 2, 2017 from https://health.gov/dietaryguidelines/2015 /resources/2015-2020_Dietary_Guidelines.pdf.

5. Harvard Medical School, *HEALTHbeat: 20 No-Sweat Ways to Get More Exercise*, Boston, Harvard Health Publications, October 14, 2008.

6. Tom Rath, *Eat Move Sleep: How Small Choices Lead to Big Changes* (The United States: Mission Day, 2013).

CHAPTER 10

1. K. Anders Ericsson, et al., "The Making of an Expert," *Harvard Business Review*, July-August 2007, accessed April 2, 2017 from https://hbr.org/2007/07/the-making-of-an-expert.

2. Steve Martin quoted in Cal Newport, *So Good They Can't Ignore You: Why Skills Trump Passion in the Quest for the Work You Love* (New York: Business Plus, 2012).

3. Daniel Pink, *Drive: The Surprising Truth About What Motivates Us* (New York: Riverhead, 2009).

Additional Reading

BOOKS

Allen, David. *Getting Things Done: The Art of Stress-Free Productivity.* New York: Penguin, 2015.

Belsky, Scott. *Making Ideas Happen: Overcoming the Obstacles Between Vision and Reality.* New York: Portfolio, 2010.

Bolles, Richard N. *What Color Is Your Parachute? A Practical Manual for Job-Hunters and Career-Changers.* Berkeley, CA: Ten Speed, updated annually.

Brown, Peter C., Henry L. Roediger III, and Mark A. McDaniel. *Make It Stick: The Science of Successful Learning.* Cambridge, MA: Harvard University Press, 2014.

Colvin, George. *Talent Is Overrated: What Really Separates World-Class Performers from Everybody Else.* New York: Portfolio, 2008.

Coplin, Bill. *10 Things Employers Want You to Learn in College: The Know-How You Need to Succeed.* Berkeley, CA: Ten Speed, 2012.

Covey, Stephen R. *The Seven Habits of Highly Effective People: Powerful Lessons in Personal Change.* New York: Simon & Schuster, 1989.

Cushman, Kathleen. *First in the Family: Advice About College from First-Generation Students.* Providence, RI: Next Generation Press, 2006.

Davis, Deborah. *The Adult Learner's Companion,* Second Edition. Boston, MA: Cengage, 2012.

Downing, Skip. *On Course: Strategies for Creating Success in College and in Life,* Eighth Edition. Boston: Cengage, 2017.

Dweck, Carol. *Mindset: The New Psychology of Success.* New York: Ballantine, 2016.

Ellis, Dave. *Becoming a Master Student,* Sixteenth Edition. Boston: Cengage, 2018.

Ellis, Dave. *From Master Student to Master Employee,* Fifth Edition. Boston: Cengage, 2017.

Greene, Susan D., and Melanie C. L. Martel. *The Ultimate Job Hunter's Guidebook,* Seventh Edition. Boston: Cengage, 2015.

Hoffman, Reid and Ben Casnocha. *The Start-up of You: Adapt to the Future, Invest in Yourself, and Transform Your Career.* New York: Crown Business, 2012.

Kaufman, Josh. *The Personal MBA: Master the Art of Business.* New York: Penguin, 2012.

Kaufman, Josh. *The First 20 Hours: How to Learn Anything Fast.* New York: Penguin, 2013.

Newport, Cal. *Deep Work: Rules for Focused Success in a Distracted World.* New York: Hachette, 2016.

Newport, Cal. *How to Win at College.* New York: Random House, 2005.

Newport, Cal. *So Good They Can't Ignore You: Why Skills Trump Passion in the Quest for Work That You Love.* New York: Business Plus, 2012.

Nolting, Paul D. *Math Study Skills Workbook.* Boston: Cengage, 2016.

Pink, Daniel. *To Sell Is Human: The Surprising Truth About Moving Others.* New York: Penguin, 2012.

Robinson, Adam. *What Smart Students Know: Maximum Grades, Optimum Learning, Minimum Time.* New York: Crown, 1993.

Sethi, Ramit. *I Will Teach You To Be Rich.* New York: Workman, 2009

Toft, Doug, ed. *Master Student Guide to Academic Success.* Boston: Cengage, 2005.

Watkins, Ryan, and Michael Corry. *E-learning Companion: A Student's Guide to Online Success,* Fourth Edition. Boston: Cengage, 2014.

Wurman, Richard Saul. *Information Anxiety 2.* Indianapolis: QUE, 2001.

WEBSITES

Brain Pickings
brainpickings.org
Cross-disciplinary learning and creative thinking

College Info Geek
https://collegeinfogeek.com
Strategies for succeeding in college

Funding Education Beyond High School: The Guide to Federal Student Aid
https://studentaid.ed.gov/sa/
Information from the U.S. Department of Education, updated yearly

I Will Teach You To Be Rich
iwillteachyoutoberich.com
Taking charge of your money and finding your dream job

JobHuntersBible.com
jobhuntersbible.com
Resources from Richard Bolles, author of What Color Is Your Parachute? A Practical Manual for Job-Hunters and Career-Changers

lifehacker
lifehacker.com
Tips for success at school, work, and at home, geared to people interested in technology

Open Culture
openculture.com
Links to free ebooks, audiobooks, videos, and courses for lifelong learning

Praxis: The Future of Productivity
https://praxis.fortelabs.co
Success strategies for knowledge workers in the twenty-first century

Study Hacks Blog
calnewport.com/blog
Succeeding in school and planning your life, from Cal Newport, author of Deep Work: Rules for Focused Success in a Distracted World, How to Win at College *and* So Good They Can't Ignore You: Why Skills Trump Passion in the Quest for Work You Love

Tiny Habits
http://tinyhabits.com
Simple, research-backed strategies for habit change from Dr. B.J. Fogg, Stanford University

Index

A

Abbreviations, 61
  Do you have a minute?, 59
ABCs of heart health, 129
Abstract conceptualization, 17, 18, 21
Academic advisors, 3
  questions for, 4, 7
Action
  and goal setting, 33
  of the master student, 9
Active experimentation, 17, 18, 21
Addiction, 136
Adjectives, in note taking, 58
Adverbs, in note taking, 58
Advisors. *See* Academic advisors
Alcohol and health, 136
Alcoholics Anonymous (AA), 122, 136
Alcohol use disorder, 136
All-or-nothing thinking, 102
Alphabetical order, 73
American Management Association, 144
Analyzing, 98
Anorexia nervosa, 131
Applying ideas, 98
Arguments in logic, 100
Articles in the text, 6–7
Asking for help, 49
Assertions, 100
Association, as memory technique, 72–73
Assumptions, unstated, 100
Attendance in classes, 3
Attitudes, checking your, 99
Authority, appealing to, 102

B

Begging a question, 102
Behaviors and beliefs and health, 129–130
Be here now (power process), 2
Bias, evaluating, 89
Bloom, Benjamin, 98
Bloom's taxonomy, 98
Body scan, 133
Bracketing, 58
Brainstorming, 122
Bulimia, 131
Burka, Jane, 36
Businesses, starting, 37

C

Calendars, 34
Capital letters in note taking, 61
Career, choosing a, 147–148
  Discovery Wheel, 12, 152, 156
  Do you have a minute?, 139, 148
  hidden job markets, 150
  and learning styles, 25–26
  and major choice, 145
  by not planning, 148
  work ethic, 149
Carelessness, and errors on tests, 75
Caring nature, 6
Carr, Nicholas, 90
Categories, organization with, 73
Centers for Disease Control and Prevention, 129
Checklists, 67, 70, 93

Children, reading near, 49
Choose your conversations and your community
  (power process), 110
Choosing success, 26
Chronological order, 73
Chunking information, 72
Civility in the classroom, 114–115
Classes
  attendance in, 3
  participation in, 79
  unrelated to major, 155
Classroom civility, 114–115
Collaboration, 144
Collectivist cultures, 118–119
Commitments, 34
Common ground, 119
Communication
  in conflict, 121–122
  Discovery Wheel, 12, 108, 152
  skills for, 113, 143, 144
  with teachers, 116
Communication orientation, 107
Community, choosing, 110
Competence, 5
Concept mapping, 61–62, 106
Conclusions, jumping to, 101–102
Concrete experience, 17, 21
Conflict, 121–122
Confusion, overcoming, 48–50
Content
  in research, 86
  in teaching, 117
Continuous learning, 155
Conversations
  choosing, 110
  nonverbal messages, 112, 113
Cornell format, 60, 62
Counseling, benefits of, 155
Courageousness, 5
Course evaluations, 117
Creating ideas, 98, 103–104
Creative thinking, 89, 144
  Do you have a minute?, 97
Creativity, 6
Credit card usage, 39
Critical thinking, 89, 144
  Do you have a minute?, 102
  and knowledge, 97, 100
  questioning to develop, 98–101
  as survival skill, 97
Cue column in note taking, 60
Curation, 93
Cyberbullying, preventing, 119

D

Daily reviews, 35
Data, defined, 83
Decisions, 124
Declare what you want, 7
Deductive reasoning, 100
Deep Web, 87–88
Detach (power process), 68
Diets and health, 130–131
Discomfort
  and learning styles, 25
  of the master student, 6, 8, 9
Discover what you want (power process), 2

Discovery, intention, action, 8
Discovery statements, 8
  continuous learning and, 155
  emotions, triggering strong, 124
  excuses, noticing and letting go, 71
  help, asking for, 134
  and intention statements, 74
  major, choosing a, 146
  muscle reading, experimenting with, 47
  note taking, 65
  presentation skills, 107
  saying no, 120
  technology, impact of, 90–91
Discovery Wheel, 10–13, 151–154
  and learning styles, 27
  purpose of, 7
Discrimination, speaking against, 119
Distractions
  releasing, 111
  taking notes, 56–57
Diversity
  embracing, 115
  and relationships, 118–119
Doing (active experimentation), 17, 18, 21
Do you have a minute? suggestions
  abbreviations, list of, 59
  advisor, questions for, 4, 7
  careers, 139, 148
  completing a project or assignment, 15
  creative thinking, 97
  critical thinking, 102
  exercising, 132
  food choices, 131
  graphic organizers, 74
  group projects, 125
  habits, positive, 9, 14
  health, 127, 131, 137
  ideas, capturing, 104
  information literacy, 81, 94
  learning styles, 18, 27
  library services, 88
  majors, 139
  memory and test taking, 80
  muscle reading, 43
  note taking, 53, 58, 66, 86
  problems, unresolved, 1
  reading skills, 51
  relationship building, 109, 113, 117, 122, 126
  stress reduction, 133
  study checklist, 67
  successes, recognizing, 141
  test preparation, 71, 76, 80, 101
  time and money management, 35, 36, 39, 156
  uncivil behavior, 115
  vocabulary building, 41
  writing a paper, 95, 108
Drafts, writing, 105
Drugs and health, 136
Duhigg, Charles, 14

E

Eating disorders, 131
*Eat Move Sleep: How Small Choices Lead to Big
  Changes* (Rath), 132
Effective writing, 104–106
Elaboration, as memory technique, 73
Embrace the new (power process), 96